Praise for *Rich Woman, Poor Woman*

'Every woman should read this book. Buy it for your female relatives and friends! The style is fun and easy to read, with Pascale using analogy, metaphor and storytelling to bring the dry subject of superannuation to life. These tips and tricks are life-changing. *Rich Woman, Poor Woman* gets right to the heart of the gendered nature of our relationship with money and the structural causes of the superannuation gap. This is an essential handbook for anyone who cares about a fairer future.'

Tracey Spicer AM, multiple Walkley Award–winning author, journalist and broadcaster

'Anyone who wants long-term financial security should read *Rich Woman, Poor Woman*. Why? because it sheds light on one of the most critical financial tools available for securing a comfortable and financially independent retirement – superannuation. With so many women facing poverty in retirement, this book is a crucial guide to understanding how you can take practical steps which can make the difference between retiring rich and financially secure or relying on government support with financial stress and possibly a miserable existence.

'*Rich Woman, Poor Woman* serves as an urgent call to action, emphasising that there is no time to waste: today you must get started. Regardless of your current financial situation, now is the time to take control of your superannuation. *Rich Woman, Poor Woman* provides not only the "why" but also the "how", offering practical ideas on how women can maximise their superannuation and create lasting financial security. It is an empowering read for anyone wanting to safeguard their financial future.'

Canna Campbell, host of SugarMammaTV

'If you thought a book about superannuation couldn't be fun or make you smile while teaching crucial lessons to help secure your financial health, then give this a try! Brilliant read.'

Dr Bronwyn King AO, CEO Tobacco Free Portfolios

T0359497

From overwhelm to in control –
how to plan for your financial security

RICH WOMAN POOR WOMAN

Pascale Helyar-Moray OAM

MAJOR
STREET

About the author

Pascale Helyar-Moray has 25 years of financial services marketing and brand-building experience. She has held senior marketing roles for JPMorgan Asset Management, BT Financial Group and BNP Paribas. More recently, Pascale has been involved in start-ups and was voted Female Fintech Leader of the Year 2024. Her advisory experience includes ResMed Ventures, Investment NSW and the Australian Gender Equality Council.

In recognition of her work to improve the gender pay gap and superannuation gap, Pascale founded Grow My Money, a brilliant way that women who take breaks from the paid workforce can continue to contribute to their long-term financial security. Grow My Money is a platform where members can shop with scores of major Australian brands – including Big W, Lululemon, Chemist Warehouse, Myer, Freedom, The Iconic – and receive a cashback into their mortgage or superannuation account.

As a result of her work to improve women's financial situations, Pascale was awarded the Medal of the Order of Australia in the Australia Day 2024 Honours List for service to business and to women's affairs.

First published in 2024 by Major Street Publishing Pty Ltd
info@majorstreet.com.au | majorstreet.com.au

© Pascale Helyar-Moray OAM 2024
The moral rights of the author have been asserted.

 A catalogue record for this book is available
from the National Library of Australia

Printed book ISBN: 978-1-923186-23-1
Ebook ISBN: 978-1-923186-24-8

Cover design by Typography Studio
Internal design by Production Works
Printed in Australia by Griffin Press

10 9 8 7 6 5 4 3 2 1

Disclaimer

The material in this publication is in the nature of general comment only, and neither purports nor intends to be advice. Readers should not act on the basis of any matter in this publication without considering (and if appropriate taking) professional advice with due regard to their own particular circumstances. The author and publisher expressly disclaim all and any liability to any person, whether a purchaser of this publication or not, in respect of anything and the consequences of anything done or omitted to be done by any such person in reliance, whether whole or partial, upon the whole or any part of the contents of this publication.

Contents

Introduction

Rich woman or poor woman – the choice is yours

'Hello, how are you? Lovely to meet you.' Say these words to yourself as you look in the mirror, as if you're someone else meeting you for the first time. Think about the words you would use to describe yourself in the third person – perhaps 'brown hair, tall, a friendly face'. Now visualise what that face might look like five, ten or 20 years from now – I know, conjuring up 'future you' can be a bit challenging. Even more tricky, though, could be imagining yourself in retirement. Retirement happens at different times for different people, so you might be in your 50s, 60s or 70s; I want you to pick just one of these ages for now and think about your possible lifestyle. Speaking of physical appearance, how's your health in retirement? Does it affect where and how you live, your activities and so on?

All these questions and so few answers! You simply have so many unknowns, and so many aspects outside of your control when it comes to your retirement. For more help visualising you – and your lifestyle – in the future, see the exercise on page 3.

However, when thinking about your retirement, one question is key – will you be a 'rich' woman, or a 'poor' woman?

Now, I don't want to generalise too much just as you've started reading but, in general, rich women think ahead to their retirement years. They have a long-term view of life. They have thought about what types of activities will fill their days, where they will be living and with whom, and how they will be able to afford their chosen lifestyle.

Sticking to our generalisations, poor women have not thought about their future in this way. They are living day to day, doing their best to look after themselves and their families, and largely hoping or praying that things will just kind of work themselves out in their later years.

Please note that although I refer to 'rich' women throughout the book, I know this means different things to different people. When I refer to being 'rich', to me this means being comfortable and living a satisfying life that offers choice. Good health, reduced stress, great friends and a happy family all contribute to a 'rich' life. A rich life does not necessarily mean you have a mountain of cash to spare – but it *is* a life where your choices aren't limited by your financial circumstances.

Thinking about the future is hard when you're struggling with the present. I get it. I really do. I vividly remember a chapter in my life when I was juggling three children aged five years and under – two of whom were twins – a torn disc in my back, a house renovation and a dying family member. I was sometimes so exhausted from all the caring for others each and every day that I would find myself curled in the foetal position by 6 o'clock every evening. I had no capacity for thinking beyond the next day or week (at the most), let alone about my retirement.

But it's imperative you think ahead, because the stark truth is that one in six women in Australia retires in poverty. Yes, read that sentence again. Even more startling is that if you retire as a single woman, your risk increases: one in three retires into poverty. (I cover this issue, and how it connects to the risk of homelessness for women, in chapter 2.)

While you no doubt hope for the best in terms of having a partner to share your retirement years with, you really do have to plan for the worst. Relying on a partner's superannuation as your retirement life raft isn't a good enough plan. What happens to your plans in the event of separation or death? The life raft capsizes.

Visualising your future self

I find the most effective tools to help get a handle on 'future you' are visual tools.

So for a bit of fun, download FaceApp, free on the App Store or Google Play, and take a selfie. Then use the app to apply the age filter to your photo – you have the option of 'Cool Old' or 'Old'. Looking at the photo of me as 'Cool Old', I'd say I'm in my late 60s or early 70s. The 'Old' filter has me at late 70s or early 80s. Either way, seeing yourself with grey hair, neck and face wrinkles and saggy skin really gets the imagination juices flowing.

Next, I'd like you to watch a particular episode of the documentary *Limitless with Chris Hemsworth*. (Yes, I'm using Chris Hemsworth to really capture your attention.)

In this series, Chris investigates a number of ways to slow down the ageing process, including stress management, shock, fasting and others. In the final episode, 'Acceptance', he is aged artificially through the use of props: he's given thick glasses to wear, his ears are stuffed with ear plugs to muffle sound, and he's given leg braces that mimic the feeling of rigidity that comes with age. It's startling to watch someone so physically fit and in the prime of his life age more than four decades in the space of a few hours, thanks to these physical accessories. As viewers, we watch 'Thor' struggle to walk, bend and hear. Again, it's confronting – but it's also realistic.

These two exercises should help start you thinking further ahead – and so will this book.

A book about the broccoli of personal finance

I don't think I've ever seen a cookbook solely about broccoli. Even though broccoli is a super food, contains vitamins A, C, E and K, provides fibre and folate, and is remarkably versatile, it's just not what you want to talk about much, or offer up as the star ingredient at your next dinner party. Even the Health Research Institute of Australia, in describing how broccoli plays a key role in maintaining healthy heart function, regulating blood pressure and assisting metabolic processes, acknowledges it's an 'underrated' veggie.

Well, this book is to personal finance what broccoli is to cookery books. I'm not offering strategies to get rich quickly, with minimal effort. Instead, I outline a plan for getting rich slowly by maximising superannuation. There, I said it! This is a book about superannuation. The topic contains such off-putting words as 'preservation', 'sacrifice' and 'hardship'. I know, worse than broccoli maybe. But stay with me.

Superannuation is the mechanism by which you save money for your future, so that when you decide to stop working, you will be able to fund the lifestyle you want to enjoy. Essentially, your superannuation contributions are savings you make now during your working lifetime, to access during your retirement.

One of the great things about superannuation is that you're not saving on your own. Here's who and what is on your savings team:

- you
- your employer (unless you're self-employed)
- the government
- compound interest.

I could have added a fifth team member to this list – the Australian Taxation Office – because the ATO encourages us to save through super by offering so much valuable information on the tax concessions available to do so. That's right – superannuation savings enjoy favourable taxation rates, put in place by successive federal governments to encourage us to make additional contributions.

I cover how to take advantage of each of these members of your super team throughout this book but, for now, all you need to know is that you're not alone in your retirement savings journey. The team works together to create an outcome far greater than the sum of its parts.

The time to start becoming rich is now

Ever wondered why Robert Kiyosaki never wrote a second book, *Rich Mum Poor Mum*? We'll never know, but my guess is that when he was writing *Rich Dad Poor Dad* in 1997, women were still in the minority when it came to earning a high income, making independent investment decisions and managing their finances. The aspiration of becoming a rich woman in your own right was still quite unrealistic at that time.

Many years ago (not as far back as 1997 but still some time ago), I presented to a room full of women on the topic of superannuation, its inadequacies for women and what they could do about it. After formalities had concluded, one of the attendees came to introduce herself to me. She was relatively young and lived with her partner; no children were on the scene. I can't remember her profession but she was working full-time. I was taken aback when she shared with me that, aged 35, she had already done the maths and calculated that she was, in fact, tied to her partner – simply because she could not afford to have the retirement lifestyle she wanted if she were single.

I quizzed her as much as I could to do a basic sense check that she didn't have the wrong end of the stick. She didn't; her life situation – profession, earning capacity, goals for retirement – were such that neither she nor I could see any other way forward for her. Her emotions were a unique combination of resignation and indignation, but the thing that struck me the most was the sense that she had buckled herself in for the really long haul with this chap. You could tell that she was going to stick with this man, come hell or high water. Security first, love a distant second in this scenario. Her conclusion, and her choices based on this, may seem amoral or even distasteful. Curiously, I found myself pleased that she had figured out her retirement strategy so early on in the piece. I sometimes catch myself wondering what became of her – and whether she, in fact, did last the relationship distance with him. I also know other choices do exist. If you start thinking ahead *now*, you can be more in control of your own retirement and how you will fund it. You won't be stuck in a relationship that you would much rather leave.

In my opinion, Australia's superannuation system still favours the male population (more on that later), but today it is possible for women to become financially secure in retirement in their own right. And that's why I decided to write *Rich Woman, Poor Woman*, inspired by Kiyosaki's bestselling book.

You're likely already engaged and active when it comes to so many aspects of your life – including your health, wellness, nutrition and fitness. Now is the time to embrace your financial fitness and future, and learn how you can use superannuation to maximum advantage to support your lifestyle in your later years.

One of my main objectives with *Rich Woman, Poor Woman* is to put you firmly in the driver's seat, heading out on a comfortable trip towards your destination – financial security. But first you have to learn to drive – and that's where I come in.

Who am I to be your driving instructor?

So why can you trust me to guide you to your superannuation destination? That's an excellent question – and hopefully the first of many from you.

While I have a quarter of a century in financial services experience and have dedicated approximately a decade to educating women specifically on superannuation and the superannuation gender gap, I present myself to you as someone who has, quite simply, followed the advice I share with you here.

In other words, I'm living proof that superannuation can work for women.

Let's rewind a couple of decades. I was working for a blue-chip funds management firm in Sydney. The firm was very well known and respected, with multimillion-dollar advertising campaigns and an internal culture of ambition and high performance.

Part of my job responsibilities included rewriting the brochures on compound interest and the importance of superannuation. Aged in my mid-20s, I thought, *Gee, this makes a lot of sense; I should do this myself.* So, I started salary sacrificing into my superannuation. Happily, the company offered matching – whatever

I contributed into my super, they matched, topping up my super with extra contributions.

Following this role, I moved to the United Kingdom, where I adopted a similar strategy of salary sacrifice with my UK employer. In my mid-30s, I then stepped out of the paid workforce, as so many women do, to have children. This coincided with relocating back to Australia, and the discovery that local recruitment firms weren't interested in paying me the same salary as I'd been on in London for a part-time role (the outrage!).

So I decided to chart my own path. I founded my own ecommerce start-up so that I had a business I could run from home while raising the children. As any start-up or business owner knows, a focus on superannuation is usually absolutely the last item on the 'things to worry about' list. However, once things had settled (a little), I did start to think about it again. My husband and I decided to set up our own self-managed super fund (SMSF) after transferring our UK pensions back onshore in the interests of consolidation.

Meanwhile my work on my own start-up turned into other roles in start-up world – as mentor, adviser or consultant. As you can no doubt understand, the security and consistency of pay (or lack thereof) in the start-up world is very different to that in corporate life. Working in or for start-ups meant I had periods of half pay or even no pay. In contrast, my husband remained in corporate life and earned significantly more as his base salary.

Now we fast-forward 14 years. Only at this point, when I've been out of corporate life for over a decade thanks to raising children or building start-ups, does his superannuation balance overtake mine. How on earth is this possible, you might ask? Well, all my salary sacrifice and salary matching contributions for around 10 years while in my 20s and 30s meant my super balance was just as much as his, despite his consistent contributions at a far higher value than mine but later on.

You can see the growth of both balances over the ten years between 2013 and 2023 in the following chart. Note that the Y-axis markers are masked for privacy, but the pattern shown is accurate. The overall value of my super pot has still more than doubled – despite a combination of me:

· being on parental leave

· not being in corporate life over that time

· only making contributions reflective of start-up life.

My and my husband's superannuation balances, 2013–23

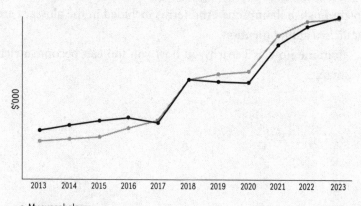

● My super balance
● My husband's super balance

I am living proof that you can change your retirement fortunes from woe to wow. And the best part? I didn't have to try. I didn't have to sacrifice any aspect of my lifestyle and I didn't even have to make any additional incremental effort. I simply made a couple of sensible decisions at an early age and then let automation – and time – do the rest.

Don't worry if you're picking this book up in your 40s, 50s or 60s. Every woman's situation is different, and that's why I encourage you through the book to chart your own course. You will be required to do some of the work. You'll find some questions to ponder and tables to fill in, to help you create your own strategy to reach your financial goals.

In this book, I share with you the strategies that I, and rich women, use. By following these strategies, you can transform your financial outlook from being overwhelmed to being in control, to reach the retirement you want at the age you want.

Lastly, don't worry if you hit a word or concept that you don't understand in the following chapters. Superannuation is full of jargon, but I've provided a glossary at the back of the book with plain English definitions. And terms included in the glossary are *italicised* at first mention.

Join me now as I teach you how you too can become a rich woman.

Chapter 1

Superannuation decoded

Australia has a superannuation system that is the envy of many other countries – yet investing in super simply isn't taught in any structured or effective way. 'Superannuation school' doesn't exist. Financial literacy as a wider topic has been taught in Australian high schools since 2015 but, somehow, the crucial subject of superannuation is largely left out of the mix. While some references to it may now appear in various school textbooks, on the whole we are not taught how to prepare for or manage what will be around one third of our life.

Financial literacy is very often the key difference between a rich woman and a poor woman – and knowing your super options and how super can fund your retirement is a key part of this financial literacy. Think of superannuation as a Formula 1 race, requiring lots of know-how and experience. Now imagine finding yourself in the race, having had little instruction or training; no doubt, you'd either crash, or drive extremely cautiously. Rich women are those who have sought out tuition and invested in training, so they can cross the superannuation finish line comfortably, safely and well ahead of the rest of the pack.

This book is all about addressing the super knowledge gap and making sure you take your place on the rich woman starting grid.

Superannuation is deeply beneficial to us all; it can help us live a long and comfortable life once we move out of the workforce in our later years. However, what many women struggle with is their perception of forgoing present-day monies in order to contribute to their super. Rich women see the long-term benefits that super offers, whereas poor women only view money as providing for their current situation.

To improve your understanding of superannuation, I'd like to introduce an analogy. Superannuation is a lot like exercise. While we know that exercise is good for us, the immediate appeal of the couch and a glass of wine can seem undeniable after a hard day. However, think for a minute about the short- and long-term benefits of exercise:

- Exercise helps increase the levels of feel-good hormones released in the short term.
- It improves your mental wellbeing.
- You're pleased with yourself for getting up and moving more.
- As you continue exercising, you start to see positive changes over time.
- The more you put into exercise, the more you get out of life.

Now, apply this thinking to saving for your financial security through superannuation. When you contribute to super, you feel good that you're putting some money aside for your later years. You give yourself a high five for your sensible long-term thinking. As you continue to see money diverted into your superannuation account with each pay cycle and your super balance slowly growing, you start to think that perhaps it's not such a bad idea after all. After a certain point, it becomes exciting to watch the numbers in your super account balance become bigger and bigger. Breaking through six figures is satisfying, and then it becomes even more exciting to break through $200,000, and then $300,000 and so on. The more your super balance grows, the more confident you become that you will be able to enjoy a comfortable lifestyle in later life.

What's in a name?

Isn't superannuation a terrible word? Putting aside any pre-conceptions or understanding you may have on the topic, the very term is so unappealing. Superannuation is 'the act of being superannuated', a word first used in English in the 1600s. 'Super-annuari' means 'to be old'; when we break it down, 'super' comes from the Latin, meaning 'over or above' and 'annus' meaning year. Given that English is heavily informed by Latin, when we hear the word 'superannuation' our subconscious is recoiling from the concept of being old from the get-go. Strike one to the government for choosing a bad name.

Now let's think about the glossary of terms that surrounds the topic – including a range of off-putting words such as 'preservation', 'sacrifice' and 'hardship'. None of this is endearing. Then we have the complex terms that many of us (including some experts) would be hard-pressed to define correctly; I'm thinking of 'reversionary' and 'commutable' among others. The language of superannuation is hardly something we wish to engage in; it's complex and alienating. And yet the government wants us to wrap our arms around superannuation and embrace it? Strike two!

Let's imagine we're a creative agency with a new brief from a client. The brief is to name a new financial product that will fund our lifestyles in the third chapter of our lives. The brief specifies the proposed name should achieve the following:

- provide investors in the product with a sense of ownership of their future
- make investors interested and engaged
- fill investors with the idea anything is possible.

What name could you come up with to capture this? For fun, I've listed a few ideas here:

- NextGen Me
- MaxiLife
- Future Bloom
- LifeRipe
- Rizer.

While I may not score a job at an advertising agency any time soon, you get the idea. These names variously evoke a sense of promise, that you're going to maximise your life and potential, and that you're managing your own journey. Even the worst of my naming suggestions is 100 times better than the name we ended up with – superannuation!

Beyond the label

Names aside, the very nature of this topic is challenging, because thinking about retirement also means thinking about ageing. This brings up unpalatable thoughts about failing health, constrained mobility and a deepening sense of mortality, as Chris Hemsworth experienced first-hand in his *Limitless* documentary. And it's not just failing physical health either – according to 2022 data from the Australian Institute of Health and Welfare, dementia is the number one cause of death for Australian women above the age of 75. (In contrast, coronary heart disease is the leading cause of death for men in all age groups from age 45 and up.)

As we all know, only two things in life are certain – taxes and death. It's an inevitability that we will die. Prior to death, we will age, resulting in some form of physical and mental impairment. We want to live those retirement years as comfortably as we can – so isn't it best to wrap our heads around this superannuation concept now and prepare accordingly?

What is superannuation exactly?

Superannuation is a way to ensure you save money for a point in your future when you stop working. The basic premise is that, during your working lifetime, a percentage of your employment earnings is paid by your employer into a superannuation fund of your choice. Your employment contract will state whether your annual salary includes the *superannuation guarantee* (SG) or whether the SG is paid on top of your base salary. By the way, if starting a new job, you should definitely clarify during the interview process whether the SG is included in or on top of base salary – rather than be disappointed when the employment contract is offered to you.

On the plus side – and it's a pretty big plus – super savings enjoy favourable *(concessional)* taxation to encourage us to make additional contributions. On the negative side, these savings, once made, are locked away until retirement or reaching a certain age. (Known as your *preservation age*, this is between 55 and 60, depending on when you were born.) However, in extreme circumstances, such as incapacity, severe financial hardship or on compassionate grounds, you might be able to take out some of your super before retirement or reaching your preservation age.

The amount that you save during your working lifetime is designed to cover the majority of what you need in your retirement. The government may also pay you a pension if you meet the eligibility criteria; however, the pension amount that you receive on a fortnightly basis will be relatively small, because it's designed to be a small supplement to your retirement savings. The amount of pension you receive also depends on whether you're single or a couple, and what other assets and income you have. (I cover how the Age Pension stacks up against likely retirement expenses in more detail in chapter 3.)

Many Australians – especially those working for local or state governments – used to enjoy what was called a *defined benefits* scheme, where you worked until you retired and then your employer paid for your retirement during your retirement, by paying a specified annual amount – or 'defined benefit' – until you died. However, all that ceased in 1992 when the number-crunching government boffins realised that employers would be crippled financially if they were forced to support the ever-ageing and retiring workforce. So it was thanks to Paul Keating, Australia's then prime minister, that we moved to a *defined contributions* system. In this system, employees save for their retirement during their working years. This is also known as superannuation.

As part of this system, the SG ensured that employers were required to make specified superannuation contributions on behalf of their employees. For the 1992 employee whose base salary was $100,000, their employer was required to contribute 3 per cent – or $3000 – per annum to the employee's super-annuation fund. At the time of writing, the SG is 11.5 per cent, increasing to 12 per cent from 1 July 2025.

As a result, we have a 'forced saving' system where every employer in Australia contributes roughly 12 per cent of every employee's salary to the superannuation pool. With 14.2 million people in the Australian workforce all contributing around one-eighth of their salary every year to the superannuation pool, it's no wonder Australia is the envy of countries the world over when it comes to provisioning for retirement. The value of the superannuation sector at time of writing is $3.5 trillion – yes, that's trillion. This number is so vast that Australian super funds need to look offshore, investing globally in infrastructure projects such as building toll roads or energy projects in the United Kingdom, or rebuilding bridges (the actual, not the metaphorical, kind) in the United States.

As mentioned, in order to encourage further contributions to the superannuation pool, over and above the mandated SG contributions, successive federal governments have made superannuation an incredibly tax-efficient way of saving for the long-term. A number of different tax strategies encourage you to maximise your superannuation contributions; for example, superannuation earnings are taxed at a rate of 15 per cent, compared to the 30 to 48 per cent rate (depending on your marginal tax rate) applied to investment earnings outside superannuation. Essentially, the more you contribute of your pre-tax salary, the better off you are from a tax perspective.

Choosing your super fund – it's your money

As a consumer, you can choose where you invest your superannuation. You can invest it with a retail or an industry superannuation fund that will manage your assets on your behalf, for example, or you can manage your super yourself, via a *self-managed super fund* (SMSF). This is kind of like the difference between paying for a personal trainer and having the discipline to manage your own workouts. The table overleaf outlines the basic pros and cons of each path.

Comparing industry, retail and self-managed super funds

	Industry super fund	Retail super fund	Self-managed super fund
Cost to run	Low cost	Mid to high cost	High cost
Investment opportunities	5 to 10 investment options, depending on fund	Opportunity to invest in 300+ active managers and 300+ ASX shares	Opportunity to invest in 300+ active managers and 300+ ASX shares Direct investment into property and other investments
Benefits	Easy to manage Transparent Easy access to view investment performance and transactions	More control of investments Fairly simple to manage Transparent Easy access to view investment performance and transactions Good admin support	Complete control over super Ability to diversify into property
Maintenance	No tax returns required Need to review investments regularly	No tax returns required Need to review investments regularly	Extensive management required, including tax return, annual compliance obligation and auditing Need to review investments regularly
Initial investment required	No minimum	No minimum	In excess of $250,000 recommended

At the time of writing, over 610,000 SMSFs exist in Australia, with 1.1 million members. People choose this option because they feel that they can do a better job than the retail or industry superannuation funds, and they enjoy and have the time to spend managing their own money. However, SMSF compliance can be onerous and penalties for non-compliance are tough.

Outside of SMSFs, 95 per cent of Australians direct their superannuation contributions to existing superannuation funds. These include corporate, such as Telstra and Qantas, and public sector funds; however, the majority of people are in either an *industry* or a *retail* fund. Broadly, retail funds are privately owned by banks or other institutions, whereas industry funds were created to cater for specific industry workforces – for example, HESTA for those in the healthcare sector, REST Super for those in the retail industry and CBUS Super for those in the building industry. The main difference between industry and retail super funds comes down to what they do with their profits. Retail super funds are a commercial entity, and are focused on delivering profit and returns to their shareholders. Industry super funds are either not for profit, or are for member-profit; either way, they return their profits to their members. Money made from the investments is paid back into the fund, and fees charged are those related to covering costs of management and investment activities.

Both industry and retail funds combine your superannuation contributions with the monies of other members to invest in a range of assets, including *equities* (also known as stocks or shares) in Australian or global businesses, infrastructure (remember those bridges?), property, *fixed interest* (also known as bonds) and cash. With this mix of equities, property, fixed interest and cash, you can think of your superannuation fund as being similar to any managed investment fund – but you just can't access the invested funds or sell down for some years.

Your super, your investment choice

Whether you manage your super directly in a SMSF or pay your super into an industry or retail fund that manages your money for you, you still have choice. It is your money. You might not be able to access it for some years, but it is *yours*. This is one message that rich women appreciate. It's their money and they own it – in every sense of the word.

When you choose your super fund, as well as ensuring that they maximise your investment returns, make sure your money is invested in a way that aligns with your values. Worried about the environment? Find a super fund that invests in renewable energy. Are *environmental, social and governance* (ESG) considerations high on your agenda? Ensure that your super is invested in or managed by a group that meets the requisite ESG criteria or aligns with the UN's Sustainable Development Goals.

An example of the power of choice comes from the fascinating story of Dr Bronwyn King AO, a radiation oncologist, whose job involved assessing patient X-rays of lung cancers. I had the privilege of meeting Bronwyn some years ago, and heard the story directly from her. When she joined her new employer, Bronwyn accepted her employer's selection of corporate superannuation fund. In 2010, over a coffee meeting with her superannuation fund representative, she discovered, to her horror, that her fund's investments included Philip Morris and British American Tobacco. She was absolutely dismayed to realise she was part-owner, via her superannuation fund, of the products that caused death and disease in the patients who walked through her door each week. At that time, 15,000 deaths in Australia and 6 million deaths globally each year were caused, directly or indirectly, by tobacco products.

Bronwyn started a personal campaign, engaging with superannuation fund executives and boards to encourage them to divest their portfolios of tobacco stocks. Three years after she started that campaign, she had convinced 14 superannuation funds to do so. By 2023, Bronwyn had convinced 35 Australian superannuation funds to divest from tobacco stocks worth approximately $2.5 billion. Bronwyn has now taken her campaign international, and convinced a few of the massive international investment funds from Sweden, France and the United States, all investing for their members' pensions, to divest tobacco stocks from their portfolios. (For more on Dr King's amazing campaign, check out her TED Talk, 'You may be accidentally investing in cigarette companies'.)

While I'm not suggesting that you undertake campaigning on a similar level to Bronwyn's, the point remains: it's your money, so make sure you're directing it in a way that resonates with you.

Increasingly, super funds are putting their very-significant monies into specific areas of focus. For example, HESTA aims to have 10 per cent of its portfolio invested in climate solutions such as renewable energy and sustainable property by 2030. Aware Super offers four socially conscious investment options, managed to various screens based on climate change, ethics, conventions and controversies. You may think the value of your super account is too small to make any significant difference but when combined with everyone else's super monies, it does make a difference. Think of it as the power of the collective. Not only that, but you'll probably also sleep a little easier at night knowing that your money is working where you want it to.

Working out your appetite for risk

One last consideration when choosing your super fund and investment option is your *risk profile*. In general, younger women can afford to invest in riskier options – what super funds refer to as 'growth' investment strategies – whereas women closer to retirement age might choose a more conservative investment strategy. Leaving your superannuation just in the one type of fund for decades is not a good idea – as you and your circumstances change, so too should your super choices. I cover various life changes that can dramatically impact your superannuation more in chapter 10.

Just what is a 'balanced' approach?

A word to the wise when it comes to choosing your investment strategy within your super fund: the industry doesn't have a standardised definition for common strategies such as 'balanced' or 'growth'. So what one fund calls a 'balanced' investment strategy may actually be categorised as 'growth' by another. Recently, my friend Glen James of the Retire Right podcast highlighted the need for regulation of nomenclature on this front. He advises:

No two 'balanced' funds are the same. The balanced part refers to the mix of growth versus defensive assets they've built into the portfolio, but the percentage of each differs from fund to fund. Some have a split of 60 per cent growth and 40 per cent defensive. The fund next door might be 70/30 or 80/20 – it's inconsistent across the industry. And it doesn't exactly represent the idea of 'balanced', which most people would think of as 50/50.

In short, make sure you understand the specifics of the investment profile of your chosen superannuation fund.

Returning to the exercise analogy, you've engaged a personal trainer to lead your exercise regime. You've completed a fitness assessment and stated your goals. However, as time wears on, perhaps you find that you're not seeing the results you had expected, although you continue to pay your fees. Wouldn't it be time to review the relationship, and consider finding someone else?

Or, say you started with a particular trainer when you were working at one company. Then you changed employers, and your new employer recommended a different personal trainer. Now you find you're paying two sets of fees, even though you only have time to attend training sessions with the new trainer. Again, time to reconsider your circumstances – and for more on this, see the following section.

Rich woman strategy

When it comes to choosing a super fund and their appropriate investment options, a rich woman strategy is to first consult a financial adviser. The adviser can help you get a sense of your risk appetite and what type of fund– for example, high growth, growth or balanced – the adviser recommends to you, based on your risk appetite. To find an adviser who's right for you, check out the Financial Advice Association Australia (faaa.au). On their website, you can sort by postcode to find advisers either near your home or your work. Also make sure you then do some due diligence on your short list of selected advisers – use Adviser Ratings (adviserratings.com.au) for help with this.

Another option is to research the particular superannuation fund you're already with or interested in. The fund website should have some kind of tool to help you assess your risk profile and choose which kind of fund is right for you. You can also access a number of self-directed financial advice platforms to help with your decisions, including InvestSMART

(investsmart.com.au) and Stockspot (stockspot.com.au). And don't forget the independent comparison tools to help you understand how various funds are performing – for example, Canstar (canstar.com.au/superannuation/) and Super Ratings (superratings.com.au).

Finding and consolidating your super

The Royal Commission into Misconduct in the Banking, Super-annuation and Financial Services Industry, also known as the Hayne Royal Commission, found – among a whole lot of other things – that 40 per cent of Australians had more than one super account. In fact, when averaged across the adult population, the number of active superannuation accounts in Australia worked out to be 2.3 accounts for each adult. In the past, an employee was often encouraged to set up a new superannuation account with that employer's corporate super provider when they started at the firm. Often these employees forgot about their previous super fund, and so in setting up the new fund, they ended up paying two, or sometimes three, sets of super account fees.

Of course, consolidation of your superannuation funds had always been encouraged but the theory of it was very different to the execution. Perhaps you remember the very public – and true – story of Josh Wilson, who tried for months and months to consolidate his superannuation from his old employer to his new. Josh battled endlessly with his old super provider, which made it extremely difficult for him to move his balance across. Citing the need for security and privacy – which is understandable – the provider eventually sent a letter to Josh's address, asking him to contact them to confirm his address before they could release the funds. Huh? The circular nature of this process, in addition to all the other obstacles the fund set up, meant it was over 12 months before Josh could finally consolidate his super – during which the super provider had been able to earn fees on Josh's superannuation balance. As they say, turkeys don't vote for Christmas.

The Protecting Your Super legislation, resulting from the Hayne Royal Commission, states that if a member has not contributed to their super fund in 16 months and has not been in touch with the fund, despite repeated contact attempts, the fund must turn off a member's default super insurance. If the balance of the inactive account is below $6000, that member's super monies are transferred from the super fund to the Australian Taxation Office (ATO) for safeguard. This is to ensure that the value of the member's monies is not eroded by super fund fees and that the member can eventually be reunited with their monies.

Using tech to stay on top of your super

One problem with superannuation is its long-term approach. In making super contributions, women can feel 'deprived' of this money now, particularly if they are unsure of where it is and how it is performing – in a perfect example of 'out of sight, out of mind'.

Historically, all super fund members received an annual superannuation statement – and most of us chose to ignore it, or put it in 'the circular file' (the bin). The super funds welcomed this because it led to greater member apathy. Few members chose to take an active role in managing their super. They didn't move their money, and the fund could continue to collect its fees for doing little actual 'management'.

Indeed, the Hayne Royal Commission found that all funds – and particularly many of the retail funds – had been underperforming. This chronic underperformance meant that a disproportionate number of members were reaching retirement with significantly less money than they had hoped. The finding prompted a slew of changes, including the implementation of a performance test – where if a fund fails to reach certain stated growth targets within a particular time frame, it must close.

The superannuation sector has also been dragged, with a little kicking and screaming, into the technological age, with most super funds now offering members an app to track their fund. Instead of trying to find that paper statement or that lost password for your web login, staying up to speed with your superannuation – including the fund balance and fees charged – has never been easier.

You can also use tech to compare your existing super fund's performance with other funds – for example, by using the YourSuper comparison tool available via your ATO online services on myGov (my.gov.au). And don't forget the power and value of social media community groups when it comes to being informed of the various benefits and downsides of superannuation and other investments. In particular, check out Retire Right (retireright.com.au for the podcast and facebook.com/groups/retireright for the Facebook discussion group) and She's on the Money (shesonthemoney.com.au andfacebook.com/groups/ShesontheMoneyAUS).

Technology has democratised both the way you can access information relating to superannuation and the nature of this information. This information is now yours for the taking. Like exercise, you should be reviewing your super's performance and fees regularly. Stay engaged with it – this is your money, and your future.

Chapter 2

Past, present, future

Why is super such an issue for so many Australian women?

Any good story has the past, a present and the future. The story of Australia's $3.5 trillion superannuation system is no different.

As mentioned in chapter 1, back in 1992 Paul Keating, with a little help from Brian Howe and Kim Beazley, introduced the compulsory employer contribution scheme. This was part of a wider reform package addressing Australia's looming retirement income dilemma caused by its ageing population. Under the legislation, the solution was a 'three pillars' approach to retirement income:

1. compulsory employer contributions to superannuation funds as a percentage of earnings, which would come to be known as SG

2. further individual contributions to superannuation funds and other investments

3. if insufficient, a safety net of a means-tested government-funded age pension.

Of course, Australia in 1992 was a pretty different place from what it is today (although some might say still not quite different enough).

Policy-makers were predominantly men, and still made policy based on an assumption that the main wage earners were men and/or had life patterns like men – that is, in full-time work, uninterrupted, through the entire length of their careers. If only a woman – or ten, across a range of experience, including part-time and full-time work, single and married and divorced – had been seated at the policy table when formulating superannuation. They would have been able to give their perspective when it came to the impact these life events have on their financial futures.

Undoubtedly, the male policy-makers still assumed financial planning for the household was best left in the hands of men. Perhaps Keating liked to go home to The Lodge in Canberra and discuss the wonders of compound interest with his son, Patrick, and not his three daughters. Who knows? What we do know is that, in the case of superannuation, Keating and his crew set up a system where the more you earned through paid employment, and the more you could contribute through your working life, the more money you ended up with at retirement.

Simple, right? But, perhaps inadvertently, they didn't consider what work or life looked like outside their pale and male template to think about the ramifications for your super if not cut from this cloth. Equally, they did not look ahead to modern-day Australia to see how women would be at a disadvantage within this system.

Now, let's fast-forward to our more progressive, post-COVID world. At time of writing, 62.2 per cent of women are in the workforce, compared to 52.4 per cent in 1992. And more women are involved in the policy-making process. Baby steps.

However, women still lag their male counterparts both financially and in superannuation savings for three main reasons:

1. the gender pay gap
2. the super gap
3. the knowledge gap.

Let's explore each of these present realities to understand the importance of taking control of your future financial security.

The gender pay gap

While Australia has long called itself the lucky country, its women have been far from fortunate when it comes to gender equality.

Mostly, we've kept up appearances on the world stage – and, in some cases, even started out somewhat ahead. Women won the vote in Australia in 1902, compared to 1920 in the United States (with US state laws and practices still keeping Black Americans from the polls) and 1928 in England. (Of course, our New Zealand neighbours won't let us forget we were behind them, with women winning the vote there in 1893.) And the 1969 equal pay ruling in Australia secured equal pay for women in instances where they were assessed as doing exactly the same work as men in traditionally male roles – while also establishing the general female award minimum wage at 85 per cent of the male wage, still recognising the 'breadwinner' component of male pay rates.

And certainly for a couple of decades thereafter, it seemed as if Australia was continuing to make great strides in ensuring its women were given the same opportunities as men. In 1973, a ruling from the Australian Conciliation and Arbitration Commission granted an equal minimum wage to all Australians, regardless of their sex, and in 1974 the 'breadwinner' component of a male wage was removed. In fact, by 2006 the World

Economic Forum's Global Gender Gap Index (GGPI) – which measures gender equality across a number of facets such as economic, political and social participation – ranked Australia 15th in the world.

Then the wheels started falling off, and our GGPI ranking started sliding backwards. Just over a decade later in 2019, Australia had fallen to 44th place. Were other countries becoming more progressive? Or was Australia regressing? I would suggest a little of the former, and a lot of the latter.

In the following sections, I run through some of the ways Australia is still falling short in the *gender pay gap* and women's earning potential.

Women are actually paid less

According to the federal government's Workplace Gender Equality Agency (WGEA), at the time of writing the gender pay gap in Australia sits at an average of 21.7 per cent across all sectors, if overtime and bonuses are included. In other words, on average, for every $1 men earn, women earn 78 cents.

Every year, WGEA even highlights the gender pay gap with Equal Pay Day – on a date chosen based on the number of extra days after the end of financial year that it takes women to earn the same pay as men. In 2023, this date was 25 August, with women having to work an extra 56 days a year to receive the same pay as men doing the same work. In 2024, that date was 19 August. (Look out for the date next year, and schedule that Out Of Office, ladies!)

Pay gap figures provide an average across all types of work, and all work sectors. They don't reflect the difference in pay between a man and a woman for doing the same job; rather, it's an expression of the difference between women's and men's total remuneration, expressed as a percentage of men's total remuneration. For example, let's say remuneration for a particular sector for men is $1 billion, while total remuneration for women is $900 million. The difference is $100 million; over the male remuneration figure of $1 billion, the gender pay gap is therefore 10 per cent.

What starts in the home...

Perhaps unremarkably, the gender pay gap starts in the home and it starts early.

As a nation, we pay our daughters around 27 per cent less pocket money than we pay our sons! 'How on earth is this possible?' you ask. The *Westpac Kids and Money Report*, commission by Westpac and completed by Sweeney Research, surveyed parents on the chores completed by their children, time spent on these chores and the money earned. Their responses revealed that, overall, girls earned less pocket money than boys while spending more time completing chores, simply because of our ingrained behaviours and attitudes towards female roles in society. This is perfectly illustrated by asking little Jane to unpack the dishwasher to 'help out' around the house, yet paying little Tommy $2 to take the rubbish bins out for collection.

The table overleaf illustrates how the average pocket money paid compared to hours worked, according to the Westpac report.

So with girls earning less pocket money than boys, one in two women being discriminated against for being a parent, according to the Australian Human Rights Commission, and then women retiring with 25 per cent less super than men, according to 2023 data from the Association of

Superannuation Funds of Australia, this picture can only be described as a life bookended – and punctuated by – economic disadvantage.

Poor women – literally.

Average pocket money and hours worked, girls versus boys

	Girls	Boys
Average pocket money	$45.00	$48.00
Average hours worked	2.7	2.1
Hourly rate	$16.67	$22.86
Difference between hourly rate	–$6.19	
Difference as percentage	–27%	

Women are the primary caregivers

While more men are stepping up to be the primary caregiver, and taking parental leave to do so, WGEA data from 2020–21 highlights women still account for 88 per cent of all primary carer's leave utilised.

When women step out of the workforce to raise children – or look after elderly parents – they're likely not contributing to their super. At the time of writing, superannuation is not paid on corporate-funded or government-funded parental leave. (The federal government has announced super will be paid on government-funded parental leave from 1 July 2025.)

However, women as primary caregivers extends beyond just parental leave. The Household, Income and Labour Dynamics in Australia (HILDA) Survey tracks family dynamics, economic wellbeing, subjective wellbeing and labour market dynamics, by following 17,000 families using longitudinal data. (The most recent report, dated 2022, segregated its Victorian participants from the rest of Australia, in recognition of the extensive and ongoing COVID-induced lockdowns, which skewed the data.)

Let's examine what these figures reveal when it comes to the domestic load for women. Firstly, they show that women's time spent in paid employment, combined with travel to and from that workplace, was 31 per cent less than men, and 36 per cent less time on outdoor tasks.

Yet women spent at least double the amount of time compared to men on tasks such as:

- playing with or caring for their own children – 3.4 hours per week for men nationally, excluding Victoria, compared to 7.2 hours for women
- looking after other people's children – 0.6 hours for men versus 1.2 hours for women
- caring for disabled spouse or elderly parents – 1 hour for men versus 2.1 hours for women.

You may be surprised to learn that Australia has 2.65 million unpaid carers – or one in ten adults. According to the Australian Institute of Health and Welfare (AIHW), women represent 72 per cent of primary unpaid carers and 57.3 per cent of all unpaid carers, translating to a whole lot of women who spend their time and effort looking after spouses, siblings, parents or other relatives.

Clearly, women continue to shoulder the burden of care for others when it comes to children and relatives, despite the fact the majority of them are also in paid employment.

No wonder women have so little time for themselves – not to mention time for boosting their incomes and savings for their retirement.

The real cost of unpaid work

Looking further into the implications of the HILDA Survey helps us understand the true cost of unpaid work. Let's consider the findings that women continue to provide more unpaid work than men as a formula:

IF   the unequal distribution of unpaid care
        work = reinforcement of gender stereotypes

AND   reinforcement of gender stereotypes = gender
        inequalities in the labour market

THEN   redistribution of unpaid care work can reduce
        gender stereotypes and increase female
        workforce participation.

Sounds simple: sharing the load at home means more women in the workplace, and more women earning more money and saving for their retirement – it's a piece of cake! Is it possible though? Can we take our cue from other countries? Tracking down up-to-date global data for paid and unpaid work by gender is a bit tricky but as an example, in 2016 WGEA released their 'Unpaid care work and the labour market' insight paper. There they highlight that, according to the most recently available Organization for Economic Cooperation and Development (OECD) data, women in Australia spent almost two-thirds – 64.4 per cent – of their total work per day in unpaid work. At the other end of the spectrum, women in Sweden spent 43.5 per cent of their total work per day in unpaid work. The difference between the two countries when it comes to their workforce participation rate was also clear – at 68.9 per cent and 76.2 per cent respectively.

It would be unfair of me to suggest that women in Australia don't want to re-enter the workforce because of their need to dust and vacuum. Countries with higher female workforce participation rates, such as Sweden, Denmark and Canada, don't necessarily have a better balance of domestic chores split between women and men – but what they do enjoy is better access to family and childcare services.

Women are more likely to work part-time

Taking breaks from paid employment to care for others is often exacerbated by another part of the pay gap issue for women – part-time work. The statistics around part-time work for women are quite stark. According to WGEA's 2023 *Australia's Gender Equality Scorecard*, women are almost three times as likely as men to be working part-time rather than full-time, at 29.7 per cent compared to 10.8 per cent respectively, and more likely to be employed casually, at 27.6 per cent versus 22.3 per cent. If you're working part-time hours, not only is your income reduced (feeding into the gender pay gap) but your super contributions are also a fraction of what they would be if you were working full-time. Women are hardly enjoying the uninterrupted consistent working on full-time pay that most men do, are they?

For broader context, let's think about the 8.36 million women in Australia aged between 15 and 64 years (according to Australian Bureau of Statistics (ABS) data from the 2021 census). These are the years in which they can accrue as much as super as they can, before they need to start thinking about drawing down on it. Labour force data from the ABS for June 2024 has just under 38 per cent of these women as not participating in the workforce.

Improving women's economic participation

The cost of childcare has historically been one of the biggest barriers to women returning to work in Australia, after parental leave. In fact, a report released in October 2023 by the Australian Consumer and Competition Commission found that Australia's nominal gross childcare fees had increased by 20 per cent between 2018 and 2022, in comparison to the OECD average of 9.5 per cent over the same period. Putting this into numbers, the average cost of two children in full-time childcare was $1236.40 per week – significantly greater than the average woman's full-time take-home pay of $1045.14.

Faced with this dilemma, what's a woman to do? She stepped out of the workforce to be the primary caregiver for her two children. Now with those kids aged five and three years old respectively, she wants to be able to earn a wage and participate in adult conversation once more. Yet, on running the numbers, she has calculated that returning to work would send the family unit backwards economically – to the tune of just under $200 per week. So, in a bid to alleviate strain on the household budget, and to 'save' on costs, she doesn't return to the paid workforce. However, this decision costs her – literally – in a number of ways. It reduces her:

· current earnings
· future potential earnings
· superannuation contributions.

As the kids say, the maths isn't mathing.

The key to improving the economic outlook for women is economic participation. For decades, Australia has lingered behind countries such as the United States and the United Kingdom when it comes to women in the workforce. As mentioned, ABS data from June 2024 shows almost 38 per cent of its female population of working age are not participating in the paid workforce. In the United Kingdom, only 28 per cent of women are not in the workforce according to the December 2023 UK Labour Force Survey. In the United States, that figure is 23 per cent, according to 2023 data from the U.S. Bureau of Labor Statistics.

Looking at the data, we can see that the disadvantages for women don't stop at economics. They are apparent across all aspects of Australian life – and particularly so when it comes to leadership, either in the public or private spheres.

We only have to look at political participation. Figures from the Treasury show the proportion of women in federal parliament has improved substantially between 2002 and 2023 – from 25.3 per cent in 2002 to 39 per cent in 2023. This is largely due to the change in government from Liberal to Labor in 2022, following three successive Liberal governments. (Labor party policy ensures no less than 40 per cent of seats held by Labor are held by women.) Simultaneously, the Labor changeover coincided with a number of female independents winning their local electorates: think Zali Steggall, Allegra Spender and Sophie Scamps representing the NSW electorates of Warringah, Wentworth and Mackellar respectively. However, this proportion of female parliamentarians is still below 50 per cent.

Look also at corporate leadership: according to figures highlighted by WGEA as part of their Gender Equity Insights series, women are underrepresented in key decision-making roles across almost all industries in the Australian workforce. They are significantly outnumbered by a ratio of 2:1 at the policy, board or management table. Of the 2021–22 dataset that formed part of the WGEA study (surveying private sector employers with 100 or more employees), women made up 51 per cent of all employees surveyed – exactly mirroring the gender split of the population. However, drilling down into this workforce data revealed that only 32.5 per cent of key management positions in the companies were held by women, while even fewer CEO roles – 19.4 per cent – were held by women. As recently as 2017, more men named John, Peter or David were CEOs in ASX 200 companies than women.

The WGEA data reveals that we have started to see the tide turn when it comes to board composition, thanks to concerted efforts by groups such as Chief Executive Women and the Australian Institute of Company Directors. However, we still have a way to go. In similar patterns to the senior management statistics, WGEA highlights one in three (33 per cent) board members are women, with just 18 per cent of boards having a female chair.

Making significant change for women isn't a quick fix – but, at last, we now have politicians and some business leaders who want to fix the problems.

The super gap

The impacts of the gender pay gap situation are far-reaching. In Australia, one particularly significant impact is the super gap. This gap is reflected in the median super balance for men and women shown in the following figure, based on 'Taxation statistics 2020–21', available via the Australian Tax Office website (ato.gov.au). You can see how the data diverges between men and women as early as their post-graduate earnings; the gap then increases as women hit their 30s – typically the child-bearing years.

Median super balance, by age and sex, 2020–21 financial years

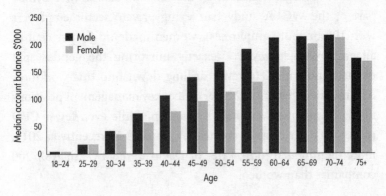

Even more stark are the following figures: the 2016 Senate Inquiry into Women's Economic Security in Retirement found one in three women were retiring in Australia with no super at all. ABS figures from 2022–23 aren't much better, with only 21.4 per cent of women reporting superannuation as their main source of income in retirement, compared to 33.2 per cent of men, and a further 18.4 per cent of women reporting no personal income, compared to 4.4 per cent of men. The reason for these statistics is, quite simply, the gender super gap.

Now, is it just me or do you find these statistics incredible? How is it that in a country as rich as ours, we treat 51 per cent of the population this way? How have we built a retirement system in this country worth $3.5 trillion – *trillion* – yet we 'forgot' about half the population along the way?

The impact of the lack of consideration or imagination (or whatever you want to call it) of the policymakers over the years has been dire on the fairer sex, particularly those in a particular age group. The older woman, defined as 55 years and older, is now the fastest-growing demographic of homeless people in Australia. The Mercy Foundation Australia reported a 31 per cent jump in women over 55 experiencing homelessness between 2011 and 2016; this increased a further 6.6 per cent by 2021, based on ABS census data. In their *Specialist homelessness services annual report 2022–23*, the Australian Institute of Health and Welfare reports similar statistics, with homelessness among older women becoming increasingly widespread, growing almost 40 per cent between 2011 and 2021.

You might visualise homeless people as older men, often with mental health issues, living on the street. Yet homelessness doesn't happen this way for older women. They resort to sleeping in cars or tunnels, staying with friends or family, couch-surfing or enduring overcrowded and substandard housing conditions, according to Habitat for Humanity's 'Hidden in plain sight: How women are experiencing homelessness'. Essentially, these women keep themselves below the radar, living in fear of the stigma associated with visible homelessness and so suffering in silence.

One single driver doesn't lead to homelessness. As with so many of life's bigger problems, older women becoming homeless is a multi-factored and intersectional dynamic.

Certainly, women over 55 years of age are at greater risk of homelessness due to the systemic issues covered through this chapter, such as lack of superannuation, working part-time or casually throughout their lives, stepping out of the workforce to care for the younger or older generations (children or parents), and still wearing the effects of the gender pay gap. However, other more current factors also contribute to the likelihood of homelessness, such as age discrimination and an increasingly unaffordable private rental market.

Research from Debbie Faulkner and Laurence Lester, released in 2020 and published in *The Conversation* article '400,000 women over 45 are at risk of homelessness in Australia', demonstrates how some of these factors have a compounding effect. The researchers used data from the HILDA Survey for the post–global financial crisis (GFC) period to uncover the following:

- For women aged 55 to 64 in a private rental, about 28 per cent are likely to be at risk of homelessness.
- For women who are also not employed full-time, the percentage at risk increases to about 34 per cent.
- For those who are also a lone parent, the risk rises to over 65 per cent.
- The risk increases to over 85 per cent if, in addition, they have experienced at least one prior occurrence of being at risk.

I'm certainly not advocating that it's possible to avoid those scenarios entirely. After all, I would imagine few of us actually want to be a lone parent, rather than co-parenting together, if it can be helped. Additionally, I imagine that if you've been down the path of homelessness before, you'd certainly do everything to avoid it again if you could.

Rich woman strategy

The rich woman strategy is to be aware of life's potential financial pitfalls – and do all you can to avoid them. In the case of homelessness, the goal is for you to understand what the potential risk factors are – and then to try to pre-empt certain situations if you can. For example, instead of renting privately, perhaps you could be in shared accommodation which caters for females only. If you're not employed full-time, then you could seek a side-hustle to help boost your income. Most importantly, look for ways to increase your superannuation before you get close to retirement age.

The knowledge gap

I want to tell you about one more gap that is even more concerning than the gender pay gap and the super gap – the *knowledge gap*. And what I mean by that is the *financial literacy* knowledge gap.

A HILDA Survey report released in December 2022 showed that financial literacy – the knowledge necessary to make sound financial decisions – declined in Australia between 2016 and 2020. For context, HILDA survey participants were asked five questions:

1. Suppose you put $100 into a no-fee savings account with a guaranteed interest rate of 2 per cent per year. You don't make any further payments into this account and you don't

withdraw any money. How much would be in the account at the end of the first year, once the interest payment is made? *(Answer: $102.)*

2. Imagine now that the interest rate on your savings account was 1 per cent per year and inflation was 2 per cent per year. After one year, would you be able to buy more than today, exactly the same as today, or less than today with the money in this account? *(Answer: Less.)*

3. Do you think that the following statement is true or false? 'Buying shares in a single company usually provides a safer return than buying shares in a number of different companies.' *(Answer: False.)*

4. Again, please tell me whether you think the following statement is true or false: 'An investment with a high return is likely to be high risk'. *(Answer: True.)*

5. Suppose that by the year 2024 your income has doubled, but the prices of all of the things you buy have also doubled. In 2024, will you be able to buy more than today, exactly the same as today, or less than today with your income? *(Answer: Exactly the same.)*

The answers given to these questions in the HILDA Survey also clearly showed that women scored lower than men across all age groups, and scored lower in their 2020 results compared to 2016. While mean scores for men dropped from 4.1 in 2016 to 4.0 in 2020, for women they dropped from 3.7 in 2016 to 3.5 in 2020. For more on this topic, and the mean scores by gender across different age groups, see the *Financial Review* article, 'Most Australians can't answer all of these five basic money questions'.

Congratulations are in order, though – you are addressing this knowledge gap by picking up this book.

Of course, it's impossible for anyone to know everything. By definition, if someone were omniscient, this would mean she/he is God (or whatever you call your higher power). And then we have the old adage – you don't know what you don't know. Although correct, this statement is reactive and defeatist – the verbal equivalent of a shoulder shrug.

I was lucky enough to recently attend a private Facebook (Meta) event at which Tobi Pearce, co-founder with Kayla Itsines of multimillion-dollar business Sweat, was outlining his entrepreneurial journey and business growth. In discussing the inflection point of where his business really started to take off, Tobi described breaking his challenges down. Referencing the famous quote from former US Secretary of Defense Donald Rumsfeld, Tobi said, 'There are known knowns, being things we know that we know. Then there are known unknowns; the things we know we don't know. But there are unknown unknowns. These are things we do not know that we don't know.'

Tobi went on to say, 'If I can reduce the number of unknown unknowns into known unknowns, I'm reducing the number of items I don't have control over and, therefore, limiting the amount of risk I'm entering into.'

And so it is for women when it comes to their understanding and knowledge of superannuation.

You can choose to learn about the systemic problems facing you as a woman, and find out about the solutions at hand. Ultimately – by taking just a few simple steps – you can have the tools to become rich. Or, you can do nothing, and be swamped by unknown unknowns. In turn, this brings less control and more risk – and you are more likely to become poor in your later years.

You don't need to understand superannuation to the nth degree. (Your afternoon BBQ conversation would likely become very dry!) But you can certainly understand the basic principles.

Essentially, Tobi's point is around trying to anticipate all potential risks and scenarios, in a bid to have a plan in each eventuality. If we apply Tobi's concepts to your superannuation, the known knowns might look like this:

- You want your retirement to cater for a living amount of around $40,000 per year for 15 years.
- You understand your life insurance will provide $1 million for your partner in the event of your death.

The unknown knowns might be:

- What will your medical bills look like when you're 80?
- If you need to move into a retirement village, how will that impact your remaining wealth?

The unknown unknowns could be:

- What kind of scenario in retirement could cause you to run out of money?
- What would happen if you died before your much older partner?

Being aware of the gender super gap, through reading this book, is already turning an unknown unknown into a known unknown. Well done – after all, risk mitigation is what rich women do.

Understand your unknowns

The most important principle with super – even if you know absolutely nothing else about it – is this:

Contribute as much as you can, as often as you can, as early as you can.

Many of the Australian women who became homeless in their 50s and 60s really didn't have much of a chance when it came to superannuation. The opportunity to earn super was likely taken away when they left the workforce to have children, and it's possible they didn't learn about super or its importance prior to leaving their jobs. Perhaps they took their husband or partner at his word when he said something along the lines of, 'You don't need to worry about your super – you've got me'. Which they did – until the marriage broke down.

Now we are seeing a different breed of working woman. Today's 45 year old, for example, is more likely to have gone to university, she's more likely to be more financially literate than her 55 year old counterpart thanks to modern banking technology and apps, and she's more likely to follow social media finance groups such as She's on the Money or Girls That Invest. Yet for all her improved tech and general financial literacy, she still faces a blocker on superannuation literacy.

Are we surprised? No. As I covered in chapter 1, super is confronting and mysterious – and superannuation education is hardly embedded into the national curriculum. Yet this blocker on superannuation literacy exists for another reason. I've lost track of the number of shocked audience faces I've seen after I've set out what the gender super gap is, what it means, and how it impacts 51 per cent of Australia's population. After the computations (accompanied by tears and terror), expressions of outrage quickly follow from my audience. A tangible sense of *'What the f***?'*

In my experience, the sentiment comes from a sense of frustration to the effect of, 'The Australian government and super industry has been aware of this major problem for three decades and it's *still* not fixed?'

Or it's expressed as disbelief – along the lines of, 'We can send a spacecraft to Mars, but we can't make super as equal for women as for men?'

Fair call.

The tide *is* turning

So far in this chapter, I've delved into the past, as well as the factors contributing to the present situation. Now, I invite you to make yourself a restorative cup of tea and resettle yourself, because good news is on its way.

Since its election in May 2022, the Albanese Labor government has implemented a raft of measures to address the various issues highlighted in this chapter. These measures have focused on unpaid and paid care, as well as economic equality and security.

Measures introduced so far include the following:

- investment of $4.7 billion to make it easier and cheaper for parents to access early childhood education and care
- improved and extended paid parental leave
- improved transparency and reporting on the gender pay gap.

For more information on the federal government's Working for Women strategy, go to genderequality.gov.au.

Like you, I hope this progress towards gender equality continues – not just with this government but for many others after it. However, the reality is that a different government will have a different perspective. And to protect against political whim, we all need to make a plan in which we are not relying on the government for our wealth.

Rich woman strategy

A poor woman relies on the government to resolve her wealth shortfall; a rich woman relies on her initiative and taking action.

In the next chapter, I outline how much you will need to accumulate in your super to feel financially secure in your retirement.

Chapter 3

How much will you need to live on in retirement?

Now that I've set the scene for superannuation's importance in your life, and why you're going to embrace building your super balance as if it were exercise, we need to discuss something else upfront.

Let's consider your super strategy through this lens of the exercise analogy. Okay, you've found a personal trainer and are working out three times a week in high-intensity sessions with them, and doing stretches or light cardio on alternating days. You're observing your high-protein diet, which you ingest at the scheduled 1.5-hourly intervals. Thanks to the recommendations of your fitness buddies, you're also consuming high-strength and high-efficacy vitamins and minerals to accelerate your readiness.

But readiness for what? Are you preparing to run the Sydney City2Surf? Or perhaps you want to drop a dress size for your wedding? Alternatively, your local netball team might have made it to the state championships.

The point I'm making here is that when you know what your exercise goal is, you can pace yourself appropriately. Yet very few women know their superannuation goal. So here's a vital question: how much money will you need in your superannuation pot to live your retirement in the style you want?

If you don't know what the answer to that question is, you need to know that you're not alone. Over the course of my career, I have presented to thousands of women on superannuation. I always ask my audience to raise their hands if they know how much money they will need to retire on. Usual response? Crickets. Honestly. I can only recall one presentation where a few hands in the room went up – and that was in Canberra, where the majority of the audience was government employees, so it wasn't surprising.

I then describe some back-of-the-napkin maths to my audience of Melbournians or Sydneysiders, or anyone outside Canberra – and this is where things become tricky. For example, the guidance at the time of writing from the Association of Superannuation Funds of Australia (ASFA) is that a single person will need $32,915 p.a. to fund a modest lifestyle. (I examine the definition of 'modest', and ASFA's budget inclusions, later in this chapter.) The average Australian woman lives to be 85.3 – so if she retires at 68, she will have almost 20 years of living expenses she will need to fund. The multiplication of these two numbers ($32,915 times 20) is over $650,000 – and that's without indexing for inflation.

When articulating these calculations, a glacial chill fills the room. I look at my audience to discover that most of them have a look of terror on their faces. The remainder are fighting back tears – with no other emotion in between. You see, these women are also calculating the gap: the gap between $650,000 and what their current super balance is – which, if you're a 40- to 44-year-old woman, is likely to be around $107,000 according to 2021 ASFA data of super balances by age and gender. Effectively, I have just spelled out to them that they need to grow their super balance by a factor of more than 3.5 over the course of the next decade or so. I may as well have told them to fly to the moon.

You see, these are the poor women. They are players in a game that wasn't designed for them. Now they're facing a retirement where their current super balance will only last for around six years. Who or what is going to be the source of funding for the remaining 14 years they can expect to live?

But you're not going to be like those poor women. The fact you're reading this book means you're ready to learn how to be a rich woman.

Don't be basic, bitch

Perhaps you remember the famous insult hurled by supermodel Kate Moss at the pilot as she was escorted off a flight from Turkey, referring to her as 'basic bitch'. Putting aside the various juxtapositions – Kate Moss on EasyJet, using her own vodka stash after allegedly being refused inflight service – the phrase 'basic bitch' became a mainstream reference to a woman who follows mainstream interests or behaviours.

Not having a target goal for your superannuation is definitely basic.

The table overleaf shows a breakdown of the percentage of individuals aged 60 to 64 with super balances from less than $50,000 to more than $2 million. (Data from June 2021, sourced from ASFA.) Looking at this breakdown, you can see a familiar 80/20 principle in play – 80 per cent (okay, 78.1 per cent) of individuals have a balance of $500,000 or less, which, as I've just covered, is not going to be sufficient for a comfortable retirement for 20-plus years.

To avoid being a basic bitch, let's work towards you being in the top 20 per cent, where you retire with more than you need.

Breakdown of people aged 60 to 64 by superannuation balance

Account balance	Number of individuals	Percentage of individuals
Less than $50,000	273,093	22.6%
$50,000 to $150,000	261,041	21.6%
$150,000 to $250,000	179,557	14.9%
$250,000 to $500,000	229,844	19.0%
$500,000 to $750,000	109,127	9.0%
$750,000 to $1 million	59,764	5.0%
$1 million to $2 million	74,414	6.2%
$2 million plus	20,092	1.7%

A man is not a plan

In different eras, women used to rely on their husbands or partners to be their source of income – and retirement funding. And while you may think of the 1950s or 1960s housewife as a template for this type of reliance, even then examples of advocacy for female financial independence existed. Marilyn Monroe famously preferred diamonds over love, citing their durability and ability to pay the rent in 'Diamonds are a girl's best friend'. Zsa Zsa Gabor declared herself a property collector, stating, 'I am a marvellous housekeeper. Every time I leave a man, I keep the house'. Given she divorced seven times (and had another marriage annulled), she certainly must have built up her real estate portfolio.

While significant strides towards female economic independence have been made over the last half century, these haven't been as strong as they could be. According to ABS data from 2022–23, 31 per cent of female retirees in Australia rely on their partner's income to meet their living costs; this compares to just 8 per cent of male retirees who rely on their female partner.

Statistically speaking, there is only a one in two opportunity for a man to be a financial plan, with 47 per cent of Australian women not married or partnered, according to Finder's Consumer Sentiment Tracker and 2021 ABS Census data. Of this 47 per cent, 30 per cent have never married, 9 per cent were divorced, and 3 per cent each were widowed or separated. (The remaining 2 per cent were unknown.)

If my arguments around female economic independence and opportunity haven't convinced you to plan for a singles-based retirement, then perhaps some further statistics might. As shown in the following table, in each of the age brackets of 60–64, 65–69 and 70–74 for total Australian men and women, there are around 6 per cent fewer men than women, based on figures from the ABS 2021 Census. And it just gets worse from there. (Read about the 80–84 year old age bracket at your own risk!) Put simply, you will be facing a much-diminished pool of male funders of your retirement.

Difference in number of males and females in Australia

Age	Total males	Total females	Difference
60–64	711,162	756,948	–6.05%
65–69	625,901	672,554	–6.94%
70–74	561,279	599,485	–6.38%
75–79	392,642	429,276	–8.54%
80–84	252,482	302,122	–16.44%

Rich woman strategy

Ultimately, when it comes to your retirement and whether you will enter it as a single or a couple, you should plan for the worst and hope for the best, rather than the other way around. That is what rich women do.

Before you whip out your calculator

To give you an idea of how much you will need to live on in retirement, the Association of Superannuation Funds Australia (ASFA) provides the *ASFA Retirement Standard*, where it outlines annual and weekly budget figures for different standards of living – 'modest' and 'comfortable' – and based on whether you're part of a couple or single. Keep in mind these figures are for guidance only. In the next chapter, I help you dive down into what retirement might look like for you, and what income you might need to fund your desired lifestyle.

ASFA updates their budget guidelines every quarter, factoring in inflation and a host of other inputs. For reference, at the time of writing the maximum *Age Pension* is $1116.30 per fortnight for a single person, including all available supplements. This works out to around $29,024 per annum, which is really a small supplement rather than anything that can be relied upon.

ASFA defines a 'modest' retirement lifestyle as one that is 'considered better than the Age Pension, but still only allows for the basics' – such as basic health insurance and infrequent exercise, leisure and social activities with family and friends. For the March 2024 quarter, the budget for this lifestyle worked out to be $32,915 per year for a single person aged 64 to 84.

'Comfortable' is defined as allowing 'an older, healthy retiree to be involved in a broad range of leisure and recreational activities and to have a good standard of living through the purchase of such things as; household goods, private health insurance, a reasonable car, good clothes, a range of electronic equipment, and domestic and occasionally international holiday travel'. For the March 2024 quarter, this lifestyle tallies to $51,630 per annum for a single person aged 64 to 84.

The following table provides a snapshot of the three living standards.

Retirement lifestyles for Age Pension, modest and comfortable retirement

	Age Pension–based retirement	Modest retirement	Comfortable retirement
Leisure activities	No or low cost	Occasional	Regular
Meals out	Inexpensive takeaway, local club special meals	Limited inexpensive restaurants, infrequent takeaway	Occasional restaurant meals, home-delivery meals, take-away coffee
Car	Limited budget to own, maintain or repair a car	Own a basic car	Own a reasonable car
Home repairs	No	Budget for minor home repairs	Budget for home improvements
Travel	Very short breaks or local day trips	One annual domestic holiday or a few short breaks	Domestic and occasional overseas trips
Private health insurance	No	Basic private health insurance	Premium private health insurance

The following table shows the ASFA Retirement Standard breakdown for a modest and comfortable retirement for the March 2024 quarter. Numbers are dollars spent weekly, except where otherwise specified.

ASFA Retirement Standard, March 2024

Expenditure items	Couple		Single	
	Comfortable lifestyle	Modest lifestyle	Comfortable lifestyle	Modest lifestyle
Building and contents insurance	$44.34	$44.25	$41.82	$34.82
Council rates	$44.53	$40.67	$44.53	$38.32
Water charges	$26.50	$26.50	$22.81	$22.81
Home improvements	$7.96	$0.00	$7.96	$0.00
Repairs and maintenance	$23.86	$23.86	$23.86	$23.86
Total housing	$147.18	$135.28	$140.98	$119.81
Electricity and gas	$62.83	$53.71	$50.66	$39.99
Food – groceries and other fresh food	$248.64	$205.13	$143.05	$110.64
Bundle of home phone, broadband, mobile	$29.70	$20.55	$22.82	$18.25
Household cleaning and other supplies	$30.84	$18.43	$23.64	$18.43
Cosmetic and personal care items	$7.61	$7.29	$5.44	$5.21
Barber or hairdressing	$27.68	$12.25	$18.03	$7.35
Media, including digital	$9.58	$2.80	$9.35	$2.80
Computer, printer and software	$5.07	$2.85	$5.07	$2.85

How much will you need to live on in retirement?

Expenditure items	Couple		Single	
	Comfortable lifestyle	Modest lifestyle	Comfortable lifestyle	Modest lifestyle
Household appliances, air conditioners, smart phone	$17.97	$2.94	$16.59	$2.94
Miscellaneous	$7.75	$0.00	$7.75	$0.00
Total household goods and services	**$106.50**	**$46.56**	**$85.87**	**$39.58**
Clothing and footwear	**$52.04**	**$39.76**	**$27.95**	**$20.92**
Car transport and running costs	$189.49	$111.82	$177.31	$107.43
Public transport	$5.59	$5.59	$2.79	$2.79
Total transport	**$195.08**	**$117.40**	**$180.11**	**$110.23**
Health insurance	$93.52	$35.74	$46.75	$17.87
Chemist	$50.36	$25.18	$28.99	$14.49
Co-payment and out of pocket	$66.63	$49.28	$36.97	$24.65
Vitamins and other over the counter medicines	$6.26	$0.00	$3.12	$0.00
Total health services	**$216.77**	**$110.20**	**$115.84**	**$57.01**
Membership clubs	$6.76	$4.50	$4.53	$3.37
TV, DVD	$1.21	$0.46	$1.21	$0.46
Streaming services (Stan/Netflix or like)	$12.30	$3.30	$12.30	$3.30
Alcohol consumed or equivalent spent with charity or church	$46.27	$26.16	$22.17	$17.35
Lunches and dinners out	$97.29	$50.96	$69.49	$30.11

Expenditure items	Couple		Single	
	Comfortable lifestyle	Modest lifestyle	Comfortable lifestyle	Modest lifestyle
Cinema, plays, sport and day trips	$11.27	$13.51	$6.76	$6.76
Domestic vacations	$90.45	$63.20	$59.42	$40.06
Overseas vacations	$34.93	$0.00	$22.05	$0.00
Take away food, snacks	$32.79	$17.10	$23.87	$12.72
Total leisure	$333.27	$179.20	$221.80	$114.13
Total weekly expenditure	$1,392.01	$907.80	$989.07	$630.55
Total annual expenditure	$72,663.00	$47,387.00	$51,630.00	$32,915.00

Numbers are weekly, except where otherwise specified. Totals may not exactly equal the sum of components due to rounding of price adjustments. Reproduced with kind permission from ASFA.
To check the most recent ASFA Retirement Standard, go to superannuation.asn.au/resources/retirement-standard.

While I appreciate the good folk at ASFA are trying to strike a balance between catering for the average Aussie and not terrifying the daylights out of us, more than a few generous assumptions are baked in here:

· These prices are not reflective of pricing in any metro area – unusual, given that 87 per cent of us live in metro areas, according to Statista. As a Sydneysider, the estimates around hair services, cinemas, snacks and dining out caused me great amusement.

· Chemist costs – something I would deem 'essential', particularly at retirement age – do not scale in the way shown in ASFA's figures, simply based on whether you're part of a couple or not. Similarly, water, electricity and gas costs don't quite work the way they're laid out either.

- Co-payment and out-of-pocket costs for health services – again, at this age and stage of your life, your biggest spend is likely to be on your medical bills – also look to be very low.

Among all these medium-sized flaws, this budget also contains a huge problem, an issue of which very few people – even those who work in the super industry – are aware.

Run your eye down the line items again. What do you see? Or rather, what do you *not* see? Well spotted. You do *not* see a line item for mortgage and rent payments. That's correct – the ASFA figures assume that you own your property outright by the time you reach retirement. This may have been a fair assumption to have made in 2004, when the ASFA Retirement Standard was created; however, we need to consider how the economic and property environments have iterated 20 years on. These changes include the following:

- Mortgage and rent payments can comprise up to 44 per cent and 31 per cent of income respectively, according to the Real Estate Institute Australia Housing Affordability Report March 2023.
- The average Australian first home buyer is now aged 36, according to realestate.com.au – and will only become older, given property prices outstrip wage growth by a factor of 10.
- Around 2.9 million people, or 31 per cent of all households, were rent-payers in 2019–20, up from 28 per cent over the last 15 years, according to the Australian Institute for Housing and Welfare (AIHW).

It's worrying that the super industry standard does not include mortgage or rent in its retirement budget calculations.

The standard is relied on for member guidance by the super funds' retirement planning websites such as Super Guru and Moneysmart – the very websites I help you use shortly.

Another factor at the time of writing is that record numbers of retirees are accessing their super to pay down their mortgage. ABS statistics show that the rate of outright home ownership by those in the 55 to 64 age bracket was 40 per cent for 2021, having dropped from 65.1 per cent in 2001. Meanwhile the number in that age group with a mortgage had more than doubled, increasing from 15.5 to 35.9 per cent in the same 20-year period.

These trends are best represented by the following figure, sourced from AIHW. Also note the trend shown in the figure for private renters. This group has increased substantially, reflecting those who have been priced out of the property market. Without their own properties, these people will definitely be paying rent in their retirement.

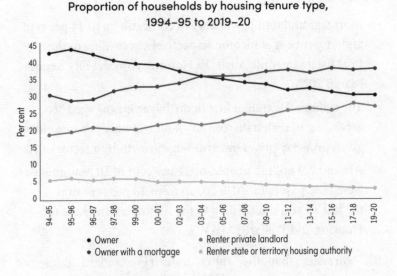

Proportion of households by housing tenure type, 1994–95 to 2019–20

- Owner
- Owner with a mortgage
- Renter private landlord
- Renter state or territory housing authority

Source: Australian Institute of Health and Welfare.

Bottom line – when calculating how much you'll need to live on in retirement, don't forget to factor in some element of mortgage or rent payment. (I've already highlighted the dire consequences of not being able to afford housing in chapter 2.)

The power of starting your planning early

As outlined at the start of this chapter, by the time most women become aware – through osmosis or other – that they require more superannuation, it's generally too late to build a super balance to the level they will need.

Let's look at this through a worked example.

Jenni is 25 years old and has just started working full-time as an accountant. Being paid $100,000 per annum, she earns an additional $12,000 into her super paid by her employer; her super fund balance when she started full-time work was $17,500. Each month, Jenni contributes an extra $500 to her superannuation as a post-tax contribution. For the purposes of this example, let's assume she continues earning $100,000 per annum and contributing an additional $500 per month for the rest of her life until she retires at 67. Assuming a 7.5 per cent investment return per annum and 0.85 per cent investment fees, Jenni will have a balance of $1,105,087 when she retires at the age of 67, as shown in the following figure. (Many calculators are available online to provide these sorts of estimates, based on the kinds of assumptions just outlined. For this example, I've used the calculator available on moneysmart.gov.au.) If Jenni lives for another 20 years, her balance works out to be an annual retirement income of around $55,000 per annum, which definitely falls into the 'comfortable' retirement bracket covered earlier in this chapter.

Now let's consider Lina. Lina is 50 years old and works full-time as a creative director. She earns $200,000 per annum before super and her super balance is $112,000, the median super balance for a woman her age. Her close friend recently divorced and the ensuing financial battle has made Lina start to examine her own financial affairs, particularly her super. Making the same investment return, fee and contribution assumptions as Jane's example, Lina starts contributing an extra $500 per month until she retires at 67. As a result, her super balance at retirement will be $695,998, as also shown in the following figure. This works out to be an annual income of around $35,000 per year for 20 years, in line with the 'modest' ASFA budget guidelines.

Retirement super balances for Jenni, starting extra contributions at age 25, versus Lina, starting extra contributions at age 50

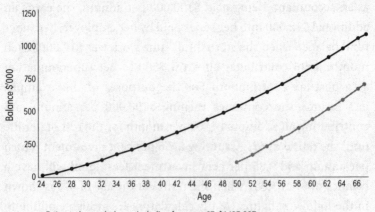

● Estimated super balance, including fees, age 67: **$1,105,087**
● Estimated super balance, including fees, age 67: **$695,998**

Let's be clear: Lina is on a good salary – twice that of Jenni's wage, and more than twice the national average, which stands at just over $98,000 according to ABS data released in November 2023. So how do we explain the $400,000 differential between the two women?

Jenni's extra 25 years of contributions total an extra $150,000, the sum of $500 per month for 25 years. However, her extra contributions earned an additional $250,000 in compound interest when combined with her superannuation balance, taking Jenni from a 'modest' to a 'comfortable' retirement.

Rich woman strategy

Rich women certainly understand the power of *compound interest* – that is, when the interest earned on an investment also earns interest. Here's how it works. Say you start with $1000 and invest in such a way that it grows by 10 per cent annually. By the end of the first year, your investment is worth $1100. If it grows by another 10 per cent, by the end of the next year it's worth $1210. It just grows all by itself! Even if you make no further contributions, at an annual rate of 10 per cent growth your original investment would be worth $6727 after 20 years. However – and this is the really fun part – even if you just invest an extra $50 per month, your investment would be worth $41,092 by the end of the 20 years.

At the age of 50, Lina has finally realised the need to turbocharge her superannuation. But it will be impossible for her to make up the same amount of ground as Jenni's extra contributions. Quite simply, she doesn't have time on her side any more in the same way Jenni did when she started.

This example calls to mind an adage I've lived by for some time:

There are three things you can never retrieve: the spoken word, the lost opportunity and the wasted time.

Lina's lack of super contributions for those decades is a combination of both the lost opportunity and the wasted time. While I can't manufacture more time for Lina, nor recreate the opportunities afforded by compound interest, don't lose heart. No matter your age, the time to start building up your super balance is right now – and in chapters 7 and 8, I provide super hacks that you can apply throughout your working life.

Chapter 4

Planning for super success is as easy as 1-2-3

You've most likely heard the saying, 'If you fail to plan, you are planning to fail'. In the previous chapter, I provided a general idea of how much you may need to live in retirement, based on the ASFA Retirement Standard for a modest or comfortable lifestyle.

However, a more specific figure for how much you'll need to live on each year in retirement is something only you can calculate – because retirement looks different for everyone, in the same way that wealth looks different for everyone. Alexis' vision of retirement, for example, may include living off the grid in country NSW, while Lucy plans to spend summer in Europe each year. So in this chapter, I help you start to formulate your individual super and retirement plan.

Step 1: Working out your retirement budget

To help you create a budget for your retirement right now, I've created a handy template – just go to pascalehm.com.au to download. The template incorporates elements from the ASFA and Moneysmart retirement budgets, but also includes a line for mortgage or rent payments. To populate the retirement template, you can either use the ASFA numbers, included in the template for reference, or use your existing monthly budget as a guide.

Before you undertake this exercise, however, considering exactly what your retirement looks like for you is really important. In the following sections, I provide a few useful thought-starters. I recognise this is a tough task – it may be more useful for you to rule some line items out, rather than decide on anything definitively now. However, try to add as much detail as you can.

Accommodation

Where will you live in retirement? Options include the following:

- metro, beach, rural or overseas locations
- with your family, in a retirement village or independently
- house or apartment or other.

If staying in your current dwelling, another consideration will likely be whether it will need renovations. How much will you need to budget annually for these? How you see yourself living in retirement will have a follow-on impact on other related costs, such as council rates and water, gas and electricity bills.

Work

Being retired doesn't have to mean the end of work as you know it. For example, you might remain on some boards, or become a consultant after retiring from full-time work. Alternatively, you might want to help out with various local organisations, either on a paid or unpaid basis. Either way, you'll likely need to consider travel arrangements when thinking about when and how you work.

Social

It's important to remain engaged in social activities in retirement; many people complain about loneliness once they leave the routine of work. Joining clubs and hobby groups, where you can meet like-minded people with a shared love of a common goal, is a good way to counteract loneliness, as well as form meaningful connections.

Consider the following:

· Which of your current hobbies or activities will you likely continue in your retirement?

· Do you have any hobbies you've been putting off learning or mastering until 'when you're retired'? Factor them in now.

· If you're currently a social butterfly, is it reasonable to think you'll continue that level of activity in retirement?

Travel

Time to tick things off your bucket list. Whether it's international or domestic, travel is good for the mind and the soul. Consider how often you'd realistically like to travel without it becoming a financial stressor. Take a look at your last holiday's expenditure to determine an estimate for likely travel costs, remembering that while some of those costs will roll off (skydiving at 75, anyone?), some expenses such as flights and accommodation will likely get more expensive thanks to inflation (rather than being due to your age!).

You no doubt will travel less as you progress through your retirement, and particularly as you reach your 80s and 90s. So, your travel budget will decrease over time.

Insurance and services

Having insurances in place is so important, and particularly life insurance, critical illness insurance and medical insurance. While costs for these may seem a lot, you can take comfort in the fact that, in retirement, you no longer have to pay for income protection insurance!

Ideally, you would also be using the services of an accountant or financial advisory firm on a regular – at least annual – basis. Navigating your way through retirement, as well as planning how to transfer your wealth to your children and general estate planning, are all areas that require some expertise. It's therefore a good idea to provision for an annual fee for these kinds of services.

Health

Health costs are probably the biggest unknown of all. We all hope we're going to make it through retirement relatively unscathed on the health front. However, according to the federal government's *Retirement Income Review* from July 2020, you can expect health spending to account for 10 per cent of your budget. It's probably a good idea to cater for more, rather than less, on this front. After all, I can't imagine anything more dire than needing a particular medication or treatment option but not being able to afford it.

Shopping and personal care

The good news for your grocery shopping budget is that as we age, we tend to eat less. And, of course, whatever your weekly budget is now, if you have children, remember that you won't (shouldn't!) be provisioning for them in your retirement. I advise allocating 60 per cent of your current weekly spend towards retirement grocery shopping. As for personal items such as cosmetics, hairdressing, clothing and footwear, these costs are highly individual. Again, consider your current spending and how much of this you'll likely maintain in retirement.

Pets

Ah, to pet or not to pet in retirement? If you do decide to have a pet – which will obviously need to be factored in to your travel plans – then that comes with costs including pet food, pet insurance and annual vet check-ups, potential boarding costs and preparation for big vet bills.

Car

Houses aren't the only thing you can downsize in your retirement. Do you really still need the large four-wheel drive now the kids are driving themselves and their sporting equipment around? Also think about whether you and your partner each need a car in retirement; if not, perhaps you can sell off the second car.

Or, you may now wish to rely more on pedal power. My husband's uncle (Keith) and his wife (Gillian) cycled all around the United Kingdom and Europe while in their 60s. Over the course of two years and a few thousand kilometres, they cycled through the Netherlands, Belgium, Germany, Poland, Slovakia, Czech Republic, Austria, Hungary, Slovenia, Croatia and Italy. Gillian is a huge advocate of all the health benefits and fitness brought to bear by her adventure; she is now Keith's full-time carer and firmly believes she would be unable to be effective in this role were it not for her underlying level of fitness. And remember also that various e-bike options are now available, giving you some extra help up the hills and perhaps increasing your overall travel range.

Big-ticket items

Retirement doesn't mean that you aren't still handing out wads of cash to your children. Perhaps a wedding or two comes up, or maybe you want to help them out with a house deposit. Is all your debt repaid? Perhaps you'll still have some residual mortgage or possibly some personal debt owing even after you retire. It's hard to know what will come up but, nonetheless, it's a good idea to try to factor in a lump sum allowance for big lumpy payments.

Landing on your estimated retirement budget

By now you've thought about some of the thornier topics covered in the preceding sections. You've downloaded my retirement template, and populated it as best you can. What number did you arrive at? Enter it here:

Retirement budget per annum – version 1:

$_____

Now I want you to consult your oldest friend, the person who knows you best. Talk your retirement budget through with them. While they will not have a crystal ball, they should be able to give you a reality check on a few topics to help you refine your budget even more. Do you come up with a different figure based on this discussion? Enter it here:

Retirement budget per annum – version 2:

$_____

Your next task is to consider at what age you wish to retire. According to the ABS, if you're female, your life expectancy is 85 years on average. Life expectancy for males is 81 years (sorry fellas).

Thinking about the age at which you hope to stop working, how many years of retirement will you have – 10? 15? 20? Write it down in the space following:

I anticipate a retirement of _____ years

Now you can put this all together – multiply version 2 of your annual retirement budget ($) by your anticipated retirement duration (in years):

MY ESTIMATION OF MY SUPER REQUIREMENTS

I will need the following amount to last me in retirement:

$_____

Step 2: Working out your predicted super balance at retirement

Now you're going to work out what amount of superannuation you will likely end up with, by using some of the calculators available online. Before you do so, make sure you're up to speed with the current value of your superannuation.

The current value of my super balance is:

$_____

It's worth noting the different retirement calculators are produced by different bodies. Each of these bodies has different agendas and, as such, their respective calculators can end up providing a range of answers. When I entered the same data in each of the three calculators outlined in the following list, for example, I received three very different answers as to what my annual retirement income will be, with a sizeable variation between each.

With that word of caution out of the way, check out the following options:

1. **Moneysmart:** This website is produced by the Australian federal government. The calculator it provides is fairly simple, but a good place to start – go to moneysmart.gov.au/retirement-income/retirement-planner.

2. **Super Guru:** This is the consumer-facing educational website from ASFA. You'll likely recognise a lot of the language from chapter 3, with regards to modest and comfortable retirements. To check out how it works for you, go to superguru.com.au/ExternalFiles/calculators/retirement-tracker/#. Note that this tracker doesn't tell you how much super you'll end up with, just whether you're on track for the retirement you want.

3. **Super fund calculators:** You have many fund calculators to choose from – I've nominated just three here. Ultimately, the super fund calculators are more sophisticated (read: nuanced) than those produced by the government or industry bodies. Check out the following:
   - australiansuper.com/tools-and-advice/calculators/super-projection-calculator
   - unisuper.com.au/retirement/retirement-savings-calculator
   - australianretirementtrust.com.au/learn/tools/contributions-calculator.

Note that all the calculators included here assume that you are employed and your employer is paying the superannuation guarantee (SG) into your super. If you're self-employed, you'd need to contribute a similar amount for your balance to equal that shown in the calculation. The experts at Moneysmart have thought about this scenario too – go to moneysmart.gov.au and search 'super for self-employed people' for more information.

What is the midpoint (the middle number) of your results from the calculators you used? Write that here:

INDUSTRY ESTIMATION OF MY SUPER BALANCE

The projected annual income in my retirement is:

$_____

The projected total balance for my retirement is:

$_____

Step 3: Comparing what you'll need with what you'll have

When you compare your own estimate of the income you'll likely need in retirement and where your existing super monies will take you, you may be looking at two very different numbers. Keep in mind that, as humans, we can't forecast particularly accurately – and this is especially hard with so many unknowns between now and then. What you think you want is likely to change.

So don't panic. What you can do now is look at the big picture. In order to eliminate the gap between your super dreams and your super actuals – as much as you can – you need to:

- **Decrease expenses:** Keep revisiting your planned retirement budget and eliminate as much unnecessary spend as you can, while continuing to think about what life's circumstances could be. For example, you might go out to dinner four times a week now but is that really feasible when you're 80 years old?

- **Maximise your super pot:** I cover this in the next section.

Let's be clear – the gap between your projections and what you can achieve through your super savings may never be eliminated. But the goal is for those numbers to be within 5 per cent of each other.

Enter those revised numbers here:

MY REVISED ESTIMATE OF MY SUPER BALANCE

The projected annual income in my retirement is:

$_____

The projected total balance for my retirement is:

$_____

Keeping it really simple: Contributing to super to build your retirement balance

Superannuation is viewed by most people as very complex. But if one thing is true about superannuation, it is this:

Add as much as you can to your super, as often as you can, as early as you can.

Remember I talked about having a team on your side in the introduction to this book? Well, the following sections outline how the team contributes to your goal.

Your employer

Employer contributions are those contributions made by your employer to your superannuation. As covered in chapter 1, these contributions are known as the superannuation guarantee (SG). At the time of writing, the SG is 11.5 per cent of your base salary, with this rate set to increase to 12 per cent in July 2025.

You also have an opportunity to make further super contributions in an arrangement with your employer, through what is called *salary sacrifice*. With this, you request that some of your salary or wages is paid in to your super fund instead of to you. This effectively reduces your taxable income, meaning you pay less tax (depending on your marginal tax rate).

Some employers also offer another opportunity with what is called *matching*. As I shared in the introduction, I was able to take advantage of this a couple of decades ago. The practice was more common then, but it's still worth checking whether your employer will do it. Under matching, if you contribute a certain amount to your superannuation, either pre- or post-tax, your employer will match this, contributing over and above the SG. For example, if you contribute 2 per cent of your salary (pre- or post-tax) to your super, your employer may also contribute an additional 2 per cent, on top of the mandatory 11.5 per cent contribution to your super. Refer to your employment contract or enterprise bargaining agreement (EBA) to find out if this is applicable to your situation.

Employer and salary sacrifice contributions are *concessional*, meaning pre-tax. These contributions are generally taxed at the rate of 15 per cent. Note that personal concessional contributions are capped, with the limit being adjusted each year. From 1 July 2024, the concessional contributions cap is $30,000.

If you have a partner, you can elect to split your employer and personal concessional (pre-tax) contributions made in the previous income year with your spouse.

The government

As I've mentioned already, with an ageing population, it's in the government's best interest to help you save for your retirement, so that they will not have to fund it. (And you thought they were just being kind.)

Government contributions include a range of measures provided by the government to help low- and middle-income earners, or those out of the workforce, add to their super balances. These include:

- **Super co-contribution:** For every post-tax dollar up to $1000 you contribute to your super fund, the government may contribute $0.50.

- **Low income super tax offset (LISTO):** If you earn less than $37,000 per annum, the government may contribute up to $500 into your super fund.

These government contributions have certain criteria; please check to see if you're eligible.

You, the member

You are the key team player when it comes to contributing to your super. You do this by making member contributions – that is, you contribute some of your take-home pay (in other words, post-tax dollars) into your super fund. These are also known as 'personal' contributions, or *non-concessional* contributions.

You're also eligible to claim a tax offset of up to $540 per year if you make a super contribution on behalf of your spouse (married or de facto) if their income is below $40,000.

Keep in mind that how much you can contribute personally (non-concessional contributions) to your super each year is capped. These caps are updated every year – from 1 July 2024, the non-concessional contributions cap is $120,000.

But wait, there's more

You can also make two other contributions that can make a significant difference to your super:

- *Downsizer* **super contributions:** These refer to a lump sum from the proceeds of the sale of your home paid into your super fund. At the time of writing, the maximum amount you can contribute is $300,000 from each spouse, if applicable, and you qualify if you're 55 or older. While this sounds like the easiest and fastest way to inject a lot of money into your super, downsizer contributions count towards your transfer balance cap, which is $1.6 million at the time of writing. (The transfer balance cap is the lifetime limit on the amount you can transfer from a super account into one or more retirement phase accounts. The earnings on an account in retirement phase are tax free.) This is also linked to your eligibility for the Age Pension. I would strongly recommend reading more on this topic and seeking financial advice on this move.

- *Catch-up concessional* **contributions:** These are an easy way for people with super balances under $500,000 to use any missed portion of their concessional cap over the last five years. This is a great strategy for anyone, but particularly for women who may have been out of the workforce during the last five years. From 1 July 2024, the concessional contributions cap is $30,000. From 1 July 2021 to 30 June 2024, the concessional contributions cap for each year was $27,500.

Did you notice that many of the contribution mechanisms are very much predicated around whether you work or don't? The spousal contributions particularly are designed for those who are stay-at-home mums or dads, in a bid to ensure that they still receive super contributions while out of the paid workforce. However, this strategy relies on the earning spouse being willing to action this initiative.

Equally, the government-funded super co-contribution and LISTO are also what I would call 'hidden gems'. It's effectively free money for your super, but again, most women – and men – aren't aware of them.

And what if you don't work? I've created a way to still contribute to your super – not via your work but via your shopping. It's called Grow My Money, and I cover all the details in chapter 12.

The following table compares the different contribution options, in relation to whether you are partnered or single, and whether or not you're working. For comparison, I've also included the Grow My Money option.

Super contribution options

	Working (PT/FT) – single	Working (PT/FT) – partnered	Not working – single	Not working – partnered
Employer contributions	Yes	Yes	n/a	n/a
Salary sacrifice	Yes	Yes	n/a	n/a
Spousal contributions	n/a	Yes	n/a	Yes
Government co-contribution	Yes*	Yes*	Yes	Yes
LISTO	Yes*	Yes*	Yes	Yes
Personal contributions	Yes	Yes	Yes	Yes
Downsizer contributions	Yes^	Yes^	Yes^	Yes^
Catch-up contributions	Yes	Yes	Yes	Yes
Grow My Money	Yes	Yes	Yes	Yes

*Subject to eligibility
^Maximum contribution of $300,000

Bringing it back to core principles

To become a rich woman, you want to add as much as you can to your super while reducing the costs associated with your superannuation account. Maximise incomings while minimising outgoings – simple.

In line with following the principle of adding as much to your super as often as you can, and as early as you can, you'll also do well to do the following:

- Harness the power of salary sacrifice – obviously this only applies if you're working.
- Take advantage of the government initiatives if you're not working or a low- to middle-income earner. Effectively, this is free money – so use it!
- Check your fund's performance using the YourSuper comparison tool available via the ATO services on myGov. Once you've logged into ATO services via myGov, click Information on the Super drop-down menu and then YourSuper comparison. If your fund is returning 4 per cent per annum over the long term, for example, while its competitors are returning 8 per cent per annum, you will likely have significantly less money when you get to retirement.

Rich woman strategy

Rich women don't settle for second best. Nothing and no-one is forcing you to remain with an underperforming fund. If it's not performing, vote with your feet.

As for reducing costs associated with your super, this is also relatively easily done. In the first instance, you should familiarise yourself with the costs associated with your super fund. Of the super funds, at time of writing, the industry funds have the lowest fees. A general rule is that your super fund's fees should be around 1 per cent – so while you're thinking about it, log in to your super fund account or find your last super fund statement, and check its charges.

Another way to reduce super fund fees is to consolidate your super accounts. For all its apparent mystery and unknowability, superannuation is essentially another product in our lives. Think of it as the personal trainer or even as a mobile phone. Would you pay for two sets of phone plans? No way. It's the same with super.

When deciding which of your two (or three?) super accounts to consolidate, use the criteria of:

- your values, and which investment options offered align best with your values
- your destination fund's performance
- your destination fund's fees.

Rich woman strategy

A rich woman strategy is to compare your destination fund with similar offerings in the market, to check you're getting the best deal on both performance and fees. Maintaining the status quo just for the sake of it is something poor women do. Remember – don't be basic.

It all adds up

To round off this chapter, I'd like you to revisit the budget you created earlier in this chapter. Using one of the calculators you used previously, such as the Moneysmart calculator or one offered by a super fund, calculate what happens if you contribute an extra $300 per month – just $10 per day – to your super.

Now write down your new figure and contrast it with what you wrote previously:

INDUSTRY ESTIMATION OF MY SUPER BALANCE

The projected annual income in my retirement is:

$_____

The projected total balance for my retirement is:

$_____

Of course, you don't have to contribute $300 per month; it could be $100 or $1000 – it just has to be a number that works for you. I'm hoping to illustrate what a substantial difference every extra dollar contributed now makes to your superannuation balance in the long run. I'm also hoping you're starting to formulate your super plan. In the next chapter, I delve into some of the ways you might sabotage even the best of these well-laid plans.

Chapter 5

Getting real with your super plan

One of my friends is a former officer in the Royal Navy. We worked together for many years and attended a number of meetings, both internal and external. He was the head of sales and I was the head of marketing, so we were a dynamic duo of sorts. Prior to a meeting, he'd turn up at my desk, well in advance of our planned departure time, and run through a checklist of the materials or items we needed. He'd also restate our planned mode of transport to the meeting. In short, he was fabulously organised and was always thinking at least two steps ahead, stemming from his time serving 'for queen and country'. He also introduced me to a variation on the 'If you fail to plan, you are planning to fail' saying quoted in the previous chapter. He called it the '7 Ps', where:

Proper prior planning prevents piss poor performance

I'm sure the navy had an even fruitier version, but let's just roll with this one for now.

Put simply, with life's big-ticket items, you cannot just 'wing' it. Life events pertaining to the 'hatched, matched and dispatched' themes (births, weddings and funerals), renovations or property purchases are all what I would call big-ticket items. With all their many moving parts – not to mention the sums of money involved – everything has to be planned out and considered carefully.

And the same is true of superannuation. Together with any property you own, your super is likely going to be your biggest asset. In the previous chapters, I outlined what your retirement and superannuation might look like, based on its:

- **description** – understanding what your retirement might look like – for example, where you live, if or how much you're travelling, and what hobbies you might continue or take up
- **value** – what your superannuation number needs to be, in order to meet your desired lifestyle
- **contribution duration** – recognising the sooner you start contributing to your super, the healthier your balance will be.

However, a key component I haven't yet touched on is the psychological component – in other words, the mental barriers that might be standing in your way to wealth creation, and how to remove them. So that's what this chapter is all about.

How money and psychology intersect

The way money and psychology intersect could be a book in itself. Others more qualified than I have written such books, so in this section I provide a general introduction to the main issues, to help you start thinking about how your emotions affect your financial decisions, and how to change this as needed.

Our attitudes, behaviours and emotions all have a part to play when it comes to how we treat money. So influential are these factors that a whole new academic field – behavioural finance – was founded in 1979. Behavioural finance is dedicated to examining the complex – and not always logical – connections between our biases, emotions and cognitive patterns and our relationship with money.

The juxtaposition seems stark: money is numbers, data and formulae. Yes, it is all those things. Yet it is also about reward, risk and abundance or scarcity. As Robert Kiyosaki famously noted in 1997 in *Rich Dad Poor Dad*:

> *Money is an emotional thing. If you can't control your emotions, then emotions will start to control your money.*

Don't believe me? Let's look at a few examples on how people can make financial decisions, independent of spreadsheets or calculators.

Emotional spending as (short-term) stress relief

We'll start off with a real-life example – mine. It comes from some years ago, while I was living in London. The global financial crisis (GFC) was well underway, and the outlook for the United Kingdom was grim economically. Some of the country's big financial institutions had gone under and people had lost their life savings. Swathes of people – including some of my friends – were being retrenched from the financial services sector. Watching the news was a depressing undertaking, and to make matters that much worse, the weather was consistently dreadful, dampening everyone's outlook even further. My local high street, normally so cheery and tempting, reflected the dire state of the economy; it seemed to me that every third or fourth shop had disappeared, only to be replaced with a 'For lease' sign. In the fortnight leading up to Christmas, usually a peak revenue opportunity for retail, I noticed that every single shop on the high street carried a 'Sale' sign next to its Christmas decorations, sometimes declaring 'Up to 50% off!'

Added to this, I was under a lot of pressure with a big project at work. Sold to me as something I should be grateful to be spearheading, this project had turned out to be complex, highly politically charged and, indeed, a poisoned chalice. One particular weekend, I decided to do some cooking as a way to relax, wanting to produce something tangible – and hopefully edible – instead of looking at a screen. Was I making a roast for lunch or was carrot cake on the menu? I can't remember, but I was short of some of the essential ingredients. I collected my house keys and phone as I dashed out the door, and headed to the supermarket, which was a mere 10-minute walk away. En route to Waitrose, one of the many fashionable boutiques on the high street caught my eye – no doubt made more appealing by one of those sale signs in its window. When I eventually returned home an hour later, my husband looked at me quizzically; I'd gone out for a bag of carrots, and returned home with two pairs of shoes. True story!

Clearly I was feeling stressed by the project and its politics, and by the economic woes of the GFC. However, for a period of time, I could forget about those seemingly unending and depressing factors, and instead reward myself with the dopamine hit the shoe purchases gave me. Of course, in buying two pairs of shoes, I'd overextended myself financially that month, which in turn led to anxiety and amplified my stress. How ironic that the emotional spending – with its all-too-brief stress relief – in turn created additional stress and emotions.

Loss aversion decision-making

Let's look at another example of emotionally driven financial decision-making, this time by Nina, a friend's mother. Nina comes from a well-off European family and makes all her purchasing decisions based on her belief that anything with a lesser price point must be inferior. This decision-making framework applies to her clothing, appliances, interior decorating, gifts for her family – everything. To be clear, when faced with Product A or Product B, which appear to be identical in all but price, Nina will choose the more expensive product because she believes the lower priced item must have something wrong with it. Nina's behaviour represents the *loss aversion effect*, described by Nobel Prize–winning psychologist Daniel Kahneman. Loss aversion describes the tendency to feel the pain of loss more intensely than the joy of gain. This results in a risk-avoidance approach. In purchasing the higher priced item, which is identical to the cheaper version, Nina's logic determines that it must be better quality and, therefore, presents less risk to her in terms of safety, durability or function.

Wouldn't we all love to have that luxury of choice, though! Nina's approach, informed by her background and upbringing, is in direct contrast to how most people approach such a scenario. The typical scenario for most loss aversion decision-making focuses on spending less money, not more. As an example of this, say Kate is deciding between the purchase of an older reconditioned essentials-only iPhone for $500 or the latest, bells and whistles version for an extra $1000. Even though the more expensive iPhone better suits Kate's requirements, she is concerned about the level of expenditure and, as a result, prioritises the cheaper model. In this example, Kate's loss aversion comes through in her decision to avoid making an expensive purchase, rather than be able to utilise the benefits of the newest iPhone.

Endowment decision-making

Another type of decision-making driven by emotions is the *endowment effect*, in which we overvalue items we possess, making it difficult to divest them. You could also think of this as financial hoarding. My father-in-law was a wonderful example of a hoarder, both financially and otherwise. A wheat and sheep farmer, he grew up and lived in the same house for 68 years of his life. That's right – he was born in the farm house and, during the course of his childhood, adulthood and marriage, he never lived anywhere but in that same house. Over the course of his life, he only moved across the hallway, from one bedroom to another. In this day and age of travel and flexible work, it's hard to imagine staying put to this extent but it's certainly true.

Located in the very centre of NSW, the farm is 50 kilometres away from the nearest town; geography and isolation dictate that any item purchased is used to its full potential and very rarely thrown out. Leftover food scraps are given to the animals or used for compost, and old clothes or sheets are used for cleaning up farm machinery. Beyond that, though, almost any other item that wasn't currently being used was lobbed into the shed – after all, you never know when a broken bolt might come in useful for some DIY tractor repairs. You can imagine the volume of stuff in the shed after six decades of this behaviour – which had also been practiced by his brothers, and their father and grandfather before them. When he was finally preparing to move off the farm into a nearby regional town, my father-in-law spent weeks sorting through that shed. In one of many memorable moments, his wife picked up a 52-year-old suitcase filled with mould, spiders and mouse droppings, and threw it onto the 'out' pile. My father-in-law promptly picked it back up, examined its functioning handles and clasp, and objected against its expulsion on the grounds that 'it still worked!'

My father-in-law applied a similar principle when it came to his investments – he held on to a certain package of shares, for example, long after they had depreciated hugely in value.

For him, they represented a connection to the company and a certain time in his life. The emotional attachment and excessive sense of ownership of both the suitcase and the shares represent the endowment effect at play.

'It's not about the money, money, money'

…sang Jessie J in 'Price tag', the catchy hit of 2010. But isn't it? The reality is that we all need the stuff to not just survive, but thrive. And how do we thrive? The next sentence may sound a little confronting but just hear me out:

Money is a key factor in mental health.

The link between money and mental health wellness is undeniable. The Australian Securities and Investment Commission (ASIC), in collaboration with Beyond Blue, commissioned research into the relationship between financial wellbeing and mental health. The subsequent report – *Money and Mental Health Social Research Report*, published in August 2022 – highlighted the findings that people who are experiencing financial challenges are at least twice as likely to encounter mental health issues than those who aren't, and vice versa. Put another way, if I'm feeling the strain of money woes for an ongoing period of time, then I'm twice as likely to succumb to some form of anxiety or depression, compared to someone with fewer money issues.

And, here's the kicker – women are more impacted by money stressors than men. Further research released by ASIC's Money-smart in February 2024 shows that gen Z women are more likely than gen Z men to feel stressed and overwhelmed by finances and money.

'Really?' I hear you say. 'Who woulda thunk it? Not only do Aussie women get paid less – even when earning pocket money as young girls – and are less likely to own property and more likely to retire with less, but they also get stressed out about their dire financial situation?'

Dripping with sarcasm, I know. But I do believe the time for pussy-footing around this topic is over, and we need to call a spade a bloody shovel.

The following table outlines the findings from Moneysmart's gen Z research in more detail.

Gen Z attitudes towards finances and cost of living, by gender

	Gen Z women	Gen Z men
Severely stressed about cost of living	87%	77%
Overwhelmed by finances	57%	41%
Without personal savings	11%	4%
Using 'buy now pay later' services	32%	25%

These figures show a large disparity when it comes to stress about cost of living, but wow – what about the topic of overwhelm? That's a massive, and telling, 16 per cent differential between the men and women.

And it's not just Aussie women who think or act this way. These patterns are entirely consistent with data coming from the OECD – for example, in their OECD/INFE 2020 International Survey of Adult Financial Literacy, covering 26 countries – which shows women are still less knowledgeable about and confident with money than their male peers.

Making financial decisions now that set you up for later life – or not – is not just a phenomenon faced by Australian women but by women the world over.

What's stopping women from having a good relationship with money?

Of course, important factors in why women often don't have a good relationship with money are the gender pay gaps and super gaps discussed in chapter 2. Putting those aside for now, another part of the problem is the way money has been portrayed throughout time. In particular, many women have been brought up to see a correlation between an abundance of money and so-called negative personality traits. How many of the following sound familiar from your upbringing?

- 'Money is the root of all evil.'
- 'Money can't buy you happiness.'
- 'More money, more problems.'
- 'That person only cares about money.'
- 'I'm not good with money.'

Notice the connection between money = bad, money = selfish, and money = problems? Combined with this, many women have been conditioned to think that good = selfless, good = kind, and good = poor. The last time I checked, however, none of the virtues of kindness or selflessness paid the mortgage or put food on the table. Even today in some cultures, the daughters of the family are conditioned to think they should prioritise others' wellbeing over their own. It's therefore not surprising that so many women don't think they're capable of making friends with money.

Let's drill into this phrase 'making friends with money' a little more, because it is an interesting one. Sometimes we treat money pretty badly, and in a way we just wouldn't if 'money' were a friend. So let's imagine money is a friend named 'Monnae' (inspired by the wonderful singer, songwriter and actress Janelle Monáe).

Would you:

- Ignore important topics of discussion with Monnae?
- Encourage Monnae to make a significant life decision without doing the necessary research and fact-finding?
- Forget about Monnae when you change employers?

If you're anything like me, the answer to each of the preceding questions is a simple 'no'. Yet that's typically what we women do when it comes to money or property or – you guessed it – superannuation.

Rich woman strategy

The point I'm trying to make here is that doing well with money isn't about what you know, but how you behave towards it. Rich women know that if you ignore money, it will ignore you. On the other hand, if you befriend money, it will befriend you. Like any healthy relationship, you get out of it what you put in.

(Almost all) women are (almost always) guilty of this one thing

'But I don't have the time to invest in my financial future', I hear you say. To help you find the time, I urge you to imagine a future in which you're not comfortable in your retirement. Not only are you not comfortable – that suggests a neutral kind of state – but you're actually uncomfortable. Baked beans are on your menu on a near-daily basis, you avoid turning on the heating even in the dead of winter, and social occasions are limited to having coffee once a week with a friend. For a change of scenery, you take public transport to regional towns or cities, because you're so worried about eking out what little retirement monies you have. How different is this picture compared to the visualisation of your retirement you developed in the previous chapter?

What's the difference between the rosy picture you'd envisaged some pages ago and this grim nightmare? Well, it's quite simple – it's time. The difference in the two outcomes is a function of the time you spend really getting to grips with your finances, including your superannuation. That investment of time – a few days here and there, a couple of weeks at the very most – spent on your financial future becomes trivial, when compared to the months or years spent living in discomfort.

And must you be the one to invest this time? Well, yes – because no-one will do this work of planning and investing in your money and your financial security for you. No-one will be as invested in your future wellbeing as you are. No-one cares about your future as much as you do. Should you visit a financial planner and pay them to care, they're still going to ask you many of the same questions I've covered in this book.

I covered the increased risk of homelessness faced by older women in chapter 2. Let's take a minute to think about the fact these women are forced to sleep in their car or couch-surf, relying on the kindness of friends and family. In a worst-case scenario, they could be sleeping on a beach or on a bench. They likely didn't think about, let alone prioritise, financial wellbeing. Perhaps they thought they would be taken care of financially by their husbands. However, plans can change and circumstances can alter – and the unimaginable can come to pass.

As women, we're just not great at prioritising ourselves. The extra time women spend on unpaid work I also discussed in chapter 2 highlights this, as women spend more time than men caring for others and are left with less time for themselves. Indeed, ABS data from 2021 showed men enjoyed an extra 28 minutes of 'free time' per day compared to women – with free time being time to spend on social interactions, going out and watching TV.

So I recommend you adopt a lesson you have no doubt heard many times before, and apply it to determining how you want your money to work for you. That lesson – heard in person, on TV and in the movies – is:

Put your own oxygen mask on first.

If you don't have anyone else at home who is able to take over your domestic load while you invest in your financial future, I suggest letting the housework slide. The sky will not fall in. The earth won't open up and swallow you. Heck, the children could even miss a bath and maybe dinner tonight is takeaway pizza.

I want you to commit to putting some time aside right now. Take a look at your calendar, and highlight a date when you can find a good chunk of time – let's say two hours – in which to get started on getting to grips with your current superannuation picture. Ideally, try to block out this time during the daytime, rather than at night (and when you're curled up in a ball with exhaustion). Next, add in two follow-up dates, with the final date no more than a month from your first planning section – otherwise, you run the risk of losing the momentum behind it all. Blocking out this time is your only task for now – I cover exactly what you'll be doing in these sessions in chapter 9.

Lock in your dates now.

My personal superannuation planning session #1:
DD/MM/YY _____

My personal superannuation planning session #2:
DD/MM/YY _____

My personal superannuation planning session #3:
DD/MM/YY _____

Now, add a calendar reminder for the day *after* session three. The reminder is to check in as to whether you actually undertook this personal superannuation planning.

If, in a month's time, your answer is 'no', then I'm prepared to bet something else is blocking you from getting cosy with your numbers.

What could be holding you back from financial engagement?

For many women, an incredibly strong correlation exists between lack of money engagement and low self-esteem. And who can blame us? Women have undertaken unpaid domestic work for centuries. Women have worked in paid employment for less than men, for decades – and we still do. Women have had their value defined by their piety or their kindness or their beauty or their sexiness. However, only in the last couple of decades have women started to make it on to the *Financial Review Rich List* on their own merits (rather than through marriage).

In short, we're not used to being valued economically. Often, we're not used to being valued at all. And this is particularly so if your cultural or family attitudes are such that women are seen as being inferior to men. Underestimating your economic value – unconsciously or otherwise – could now be what's holding you back, and stopping you from fully engaging in your own financial potential.

Another reason could be fear. Many women are afraid of what they will find once they stop pretending all is okay on the financial front. This is confirmed by Marion Mays of Money Strong (moneystrong.com.au), money coach and creator of the 90-day Money Transformation VIP program, who says the biggest blocker for women and money is the reality gap. Marion gave me the following insights derived from over 10 years of mentoring Australians on what they do, or don't do, with money:

> *Most people are simply not able to meet money reality where it is at, even when they want to. I would say this reality gap is the number one cause of financial unwellness.*
>
> *The gap between how they wish it was and how they choose to see it, compared to how it really is and what is required to change it, is the most important aspect of the work I do with clients. This process takes on a behavioural science approach and explores a client's subconscious beliefs about themselves.*
>
> *I like to use the analogy of AA. Until the person walks into the room and says, 'My name is John and I'm an alcoholic', while being witnessed and made accountable for that statement, nothing in his future is available to him. Yet from the moment he surrenders to reality, instantly everything becomes possible.*

What's required to fix this 'reality gap' is a change of perspective. If you think things are getting a little hairy now, then remember they will be so much worse when you're 70 and without the same earning power you currently have. If you think planning for your future sounds tiresome, then just remember the harsh alternate reality picture painted earlier in this chapter. Now is the time to shift your thinking from reactive to proactive. This is your chance to make a real and concrete difference for future you.

I also want to set some expectations at this point. You're going to struggle a little and it will feel awkward and hard and uncomfortable at first – again, just like when starting or getting back into exercise. You're a beginner at this superannuation stuff, and beginners are allowed to soak up information like sponges. They're allowed to take a while to come up to speed. They're allowed to ask questions to which the answers might seem obvious. And I promise – yes, promise! – that after you've gained some knowledge, you'll actually start to enjoy it. And, eventually, even though you may not think of yourself as interested in the subject of superannuation or finance or money management, you'll realise that you are, in fact, very interested in the outcome of your financial security and success.

Know yourself – and where your time is actually going

'To thine own self be true' intones Polonius in Shakespeare's *Hamlet*. Although this line was written around 1600, the advice is still valid today. As mentioned at the start of chapter 3, presenting extensively to audiences mostly consisting of women regarding superannuation and the super gap has given me a few key observations. I've not only seen their tear-filled and terrorised expressions when the super penny drops, but also noticed their anger when they realise they have been put in this position as a result of social structures. However, often a defiant attitude comes from these women as well, accompanied by commentary such as, 'Well, I'm going to buy all the luxury goods I want now and deal with the consequences at a later date. Live fast, die young and all that'. While this is an understandable response, it's ultimately not a helpful one. Chanel heels or a Givenchy tote won't pay the rent or put food on the table in your later years. And while you might earn Qantas or Virgin Velocity points in making those purchases, those points cannot be converted to superannuation dollars.

I'm convinced the rise and rise of social media platforms, especially the image-based ones such as Instagram, Facebook (Meta) and TikTok, have had a detrimental and distortive effect on what is important in life. I'll be the first to admit that the influencer life, as made famous by Gwyneth Paltrow, Chiara

Ferragni and Kim Kardashian, looks incredible. Coveted hand-bags, private jets, stunning evening gowns... what's not to love? Fortunately, however, I'm of the generation that remembers what life was like before social media. I remember when reality consisted only of the physical world, and virtual reality was non-existent. Yet any woman (or man) born after 1990 has only ever known a world with social media in it; Facebook was available to the general public in 2006, with Instagram following in 2010. Essentially, any person in their mid-30s or younger has always known two worlds – the virtual and the physical.

Consider this idea through the lens of COVID-19. Most people were housebound and not able to interact with the physical world as they had been accustomed to do. During those multiple lockdowns, most of us were forced to stare at our screens for every aspect of life – work, entertainment and friendship. Measured after the first COVID wave in October 2020, a social media survey from agency L&A Social found Aussies had spent 30 per cent more time on social media during the first months of the pandemic. Updated research from the ABS's Time Use Survey from 2020–21 shows time spent on general internet and device use by generation Z (late 1990s onwards) was highest among women, at 52 per cent of participation overall. Overall, data from this survey showed gen Z females had spent 1 hour and 15 minutes a day on general internet and device use.

Around 75 minutes per day – who's got the time?! I once attended a conference at which Wendy McCarthy AO, Australian businesswoman and activist, was sharing her thoughts on being female and trying to pursue a work–life balance. She said two things that resonated greatly with me. The first was, 'Women can have it all – just not at the same time', referring to the challenging juggle of trying to balance self, work and family. Her other pearl of wisdom was that 'There are 24 hours in the day; you should try and divide them equally – eight hours for work, eight hours for self and family, and eight hours for sleep.' While not a new concept, targeted as it was at a conference audience full of female entrepreneurs who are notorious for overwork, this sentence was a wake-up call for many of the attendees.

Now consider you might be spending one or two of your waking, non-work hours – out of a potential eight – on social media, outside of time spent watching TV or streaming services. To me, that seems to be a huge amount of time being exposed to a certain version of the world – a version that is constructed, staged, filtered and only adjacent to real life. No wonder Australia has a soaring mental health crisis, as reported by a 2023 YouGov poll, where 74 per cent of adults polled believed social media was either completely or somewhat responsible for a decline in mental health.

And what a decline in mental health it has been. The 2022 headspace National Youth Mental Health Survey also highlighted an issue with social media, with 42 per cent of respondents citing it as the main reason for mental health decline, up from 37 per cent in the 2018 survey. (headspace is Australia's National Youth Mental Health Foundation, and provides early intervention mental health services to 12 to 25 year olds.) headspace CEO Jason Trethowan argued that 'spending too long on social media is associated with higher levels of mental health problems including anxiety, depression and psychological distress'.

In taking control of your financial security, you need to be aware of your time spent on social media. If you're one of those people who spends a couple of hours on social media every day, then it's time to check yourself. Apart from setting yourself up for mental health problems, you're:

· consuming information rather than generating it
· being reactive rather than proactive

- benchmarking yourself to others, rather than benchmarking yourself to you and your values.

Before I dive into the topic of values in more detail, it's time for a quick check-in. How do you know how much time you're spending on social media? I bet it's more than you think, but your assumptions are quite easy to fact-check – you can just check your phone. If you don't already know how to check your weekly screen time hours, do a quick online search for instructions, based on the type of phone you have. Your phone can give you not only your total hours, but also a breakdown of activity by app.

In the interests of transparency, I did this exercise and share my results over the last 10 days in the following figure. What does your screen look like?

My screen time summary for last 10 days

Messages
9h 31m screen –   9h 50m
19m backgd

Mail
5h 37m screen –   13h 17m
7h 40m backgd

Safari
4h 10m on screen   4h 10m

Personal Hotspot

Facebook
1h 47m screen –   2h 33m
46m backgd

WhatsApp
6h 4m screen –   7h 48m
1h 44m backgd

Outlook
2h 4m screen –   3h 22m
1h 18m backgd

Know your values – and use these to focus your time

Why am I critiquing social media so much? Because, as entertaining and light as it can be, it is also a terrible distractor from what really matters. Social media tends to place an unhealthy emphasis on 'keeping up with the Joneses' and, as a result, makes it easy for you to lose sight of who you are and what you stand for.

Being certain about what you want and how you want to live is an incredible tool for simplifying decisions – most importantly, decisions about how you spend your time and with whom you want to spend it. You can focus on what's important to you and what you've decided is worth investing in. And, equally, you can move away from what you've decided is a waste of time and money to you.

At a certain point in my life, as a result of some traumatic circumstances in which my world was turned upside down, I was adrift. In a bid to find myself again, I undertook an exercise in establishing my values – and then making decisions based on these values. I truly wish I'd done this earlier in my life. Since then, I've made sure that when making decisions – regardless of whether they are related to my personal, family or business life – I check in with my values, and align any decisions with these.

I invite you to do the same. Working out your values is an exercise worth carving out some time for – give yourself at least an hour, possibly two, and make sure you're not interrupted. Just search 'values exercise' online to get started and access the available values worksheets. Print out the option that works best for you, and read the accompanying instructions. When you've finished, write down your three core values:

Core value #1: _____

Core value #2: _____

Core value #3: _____

Now, think about your line of work. Are you a healthcare professional? Perhaps you're in marketing or communications. Alternatively, you might be in professional services, such as accounting or consulting or strategy. How do your core value answers align with your work – do they seem to be aligned or in conflict?

The reason for this question is quite simply this: when your values are aligned in all aspects of life, you'll find greater authenticity and fulfilment. The happier you are at work, the longer you're likely to continue it and thrive in it – perhaps securing promotions and higher pay packages. And the longer you continue working, the more you can contribute to your superannuation.

One of my core values is choice. At an everyday level, that translates to the ability to choose my leisure activities and with whom I spend my time. The concept of choice ties in very strongly with what have become the four most important words I've learned in the last decade. They are:

Does it serve me?

These words have become the ultimate decision-maker in my life recently. Does it serve me to have a greasy hamburger for lunch? Does it serve me to spend time with my elderly friend? Does it serve me to meet the person who approached me on LinkedIn? Each of the questions has a very simple 'Yes' or 'No' answer. That answer then dictates my next move – in all aspects of life, be it personal, family or work.

Back to you. Now think about your values in the context of your retirement. For example, if you've written freedom as a core value, perhaps that might be expressed as 'freedom to travel' in retirement. Or perhaps it means 'financial freedom' in your golden years, where you don't have to worry about money. Or it could be interpreted as 'freedom to live on my terms'. Work out how 'freedom' – or any of your core values – translates in retirement for you. And then you can start to plan to achieve this.

Chapter 6

Set and forget habits
for super growth

Everybody loves the story of an overnight success. These stories have something transformative, dramatic and even magical about them. Consider our friend Kate Moss, spotted by an agent while waiting in an airport queue at JFK, and then fronting a Calvin Klein campaign shortly thereafter. What about Billie Eilish, who posted her version of one of her brother's songs on SoundCloud, only to find it went viral within a few weeks? In the business arena, the poster girl is Melanie Perkins of Canva, who became Australia's first self-made female billionaire before the age of 30.

But here's a secret: these stories are the exception. Actually, they're the exception to the exception to the rule. And the myth often hides the real work – Kate Moss, for example, spent two years after that airport moment working her way through 'go-sees' with agencies, photographers and potential clients.

By now, you're probably aware I like to provide you with as many accurate data points as I can. But on this particular subject, I'd only be able to guess the likelihood of being an 'overnight' success like Billie or Melanie. Let's be generous, and estimate the probability to be 0.00001 per cent – in short, almost negligible.

You see, Kate and Billie and Melanie – apart from being statistically improbable – are also what we in the start-up world call 'unicorns'. They're so rare as to be almost fictitious.

Hopefully by now, you're also aware that I want to help you aim for the best but plan for the worst. And so while I hope that you too are a unicorn in your chosen field, I'm going to help you reach your desired destination even if rainbows and fairy dust do not form part of your travels.

Another important point I'd like to make when it comes to success is this: all the non-unicorns – and also most of the unicorns, actually – who are successful in their respective careers have achieved this through an incredible amount of sheer bloody hard work. Celeste Barber, now one of Australia's most recognised comedians, spent eight years grafting away between her acting roles and her goofy spoof videos taking hold of public imagination. J.K. Rowling, who wrote the first *Harry Potter* book as a new and single mother while struggling with depression and living on government benefits, famously had her first manuscript rejected by 12 different publishers. Katy Perry was dropped by no fewer than three record labels and slogged away for seven years before she found success with 'I Kissed a Girl'.

As the cliché goes, success is 90 per cent perspiration and 10 per cent inspiration. Put in the hard work, and you have a much better chance of reaching your destination.

Planning your fitness/superannuation goal

Speaking of perspiration, now's a good time to restate your fitness (read: superannuation) goal. In chapter 4, I took you through the exercise of establishing your superannuation and retirement goals. Enter those same figures here.

MY ESTIMATION OF MY SUPER REQUIREMENTS

I will need the following amount to last me in retirement:

$_____

Now enter the middle number of the super balance estimates you received using online calculators:

INDUSTRY ESTIMATION OF MY SUPER BALANCE

The projected annual income in my retirement is:

$_____

The projected total balance for my retirement is:

$_____

I also discussed how to revise your retirement budget by increasing contributions and decreasing expenses, so that the difference between these two numbers (the required amount for retirement and projected super balance) is ideally 5 per cent or less. Enter those revised figures here:

MY REVISED ESTIMATE OF MY SUPER BALANCE

The projected annual income in my retirement is:

$_____

The projected total balance for my retirement is:

$_____

This exercise may sound repetitive, and that is deliberate. Other than familiarising yourself with these figures, the aim is for you to actually know your superannuation goal – and be comfortable with it. Remember my exercise analogy? All that training, the fitness supplements and the high-protein diet – what are you doing it for? Keeping the goal in mind helps you stick with it.

To expand on the exercise metaphor, being fit (retirement-ready) is not a sprint. Instead, it is most definitely a long-distance race. This means that you avoid short and sharp bursts of high-octane energy; you absolutely need to pace yourself. However, even though the race is over a long distance, you still need to pay attention. Do you recall ever seeing a long-distance runner who wasn't absolutely focused on their race?

The biggest strategic advantage of long-distance running is the ability to correct your course should things go slightly awry.

Set and forget overview

Every runner seeks to leverage all the natural advantages available to them. Whether these advantages are wind assistance, cooler temperatures or planting a cheer squad at the point they know they'll be flagging, they're all looking for performance enhancers.

And the best performance enhancers when it comes to super-annuation are those you don't have to consciously remember as you go about your daily life – in other words, 'set and forget' strategies. What are some of these types of strategies when it comes to superannuation?

In chapter 4, I covered the different super contribution options, including those made by your employer, the government and you. The following table provides a quick summary of all the different ways you can contribute to your superannuation – and which of those are eligible for a set and forget strategy.

Where a contribution is marked as 'No' in the set and forget column, this is because the set up and cadence of these contributions is different. For example, set and forget when it comes to employer contributions means that you agree on the arrangements with your employer, and then they take care of the rest, without you having to worry about further admin. The arrangements will continue on an 'as is' basis, and the contributions will be paid automatically until you stop or change them, or leave the company. In contrast, utilising the tax offset or claiming the co-contribution can be done regularly (that is, on an annual basis at tax time), but you have to remember to do so each time.

Super contributions and 'set and forget' strategies

Type	Contribution	Summary*	Set and forget
Employer	Superannuation guarantee (SG)	Your employer pays this to your super fund	Yes
Employer	Salary sacrifice	Extra pre-tax salary dollars you can contribute (if self-employed, you make these payments yourself)	Yes
Employer	Matching	Extra super contributions made by your employer should you contribute extra to your super, either pre- or post-tax	Yes
Government	Co-contribution^	For every post-tax dollar up to $1000, the government may contribute $0.50	No
Government	Low income super tax offset^	For those who earn less than $37,000 per annum, the government may contribute up to $500	No
Member	Personal	You can contribute funds from your take-home pay to your super at any time (up to the non-concessional contributions cap)	Yes

Type	Contribution	Summary*	Set and forget
Member	Tax offset	You can claim a tax offset of up to $540 per year if you make a super contribution on behalf of your spouse (married or de facto) if their annual income is below $40,000	No
Member	Downsizer	This is a one-off contribution you can make, when transferring the proceeds of the sale of your home into your super fund (up to a maximum of $300,000 per spouse)	No
Member	Spouse	You can split your employer or personal contributions made in the previous income year with your spouse	No
Member	Catch-up contributions	If your super balance is under $500,000, you can make contributions to use any missed portion of your concessional cap over the last 5 years	No

*All details correct at time of writing.
^These initiatives are designed to support those on low incomes or no incomes; check your eligibility.

Supercharging your super within the work environment

Now let's delve a little deeper into the set and forget contributions that can be set up so they're working away quietly in the background for you.

Checking your superannuation guarantee contributions

When you join a new employer, gathering details of your previous superannuation fund will be included in your onboarding process. You'll be required to either confirm you still wish to contribute to that same fund or select a new fund. Your employment contract will state how much super you will be paid each year through superannuation guarantee (SG) contributions. Once you provide the superannuation fund destination to your employer, they will then pay the SG to your fund on your behalf. The law stipulates that super must be paid at least every three months, but many companies are now paying their employees' super on a monthly basis. Paying monthly makes it easier for the company to manage cash flow and for the employee to check how their super is growing.

If your employer is paying the SG, this is where your responsibility ends, isn't it? Yes. And no.

The Royal Commission into Misconduct in the Banking, Superannuation and Financial Services Industry, referenced in chapter 1, surfaced what some might dub the perfect white-collar crime. Among its many findings, the commission also uncovered that some companies were not paying their employees the mandatory superannuation – the SG – owed to them. You may wonder how on earth that came to pass – didn't the employees miss it? The answer was no. The earth-shatteringly awful lack of engagement in superannuation by employees meant many didn't discover their super wasn't being paid.

And this practice still takes place today. The reasons for non-payment aren't always due to ill intention, but what transpires as a result is material. The ATO estimated that over the 2020–21 tax year, a net gap of $3.6 billion was 'missing' from the SG pot. This represents 5.1 per cent of required contributions, and around the same percentage was missing in the 2022–23 tax year, before tax office intervention. Let me be clear: if every employer were fully compliant with their SG obligations, there would be no gap. By law, employers must contribute to the super of their employees. If they don't, they are liable for legal consequences in the form of a fine, in addition to reputational damage.

Rich woman strategy

A rich woman always crosschecks that what she's been told will happen actually does happen. From your perspective, it's highly worthwhile double-checking that your employer is making accurate SG contributions into your nominated super account.

When checking whether your employer is meeting their SG contribution obligations, you're looking for two things:

1. **Your payslip reflects the correct amount of SG.**
   As already covered, from 1 July 2024, the SG moved to 11.5 per cent, increasing to 12 per cent from 1 July 2025. So if your base salary is $100,000 per annum, at the time of writing, your employer SG contributions per annum should be $11,500. Pay Calculator (paycalculator.com.au) is a handy website for cross-referencing the contents of your employment contract with the numbers printed on your payslip. On the site, you can enter your salary and other details (including any student debt) to create a summary of the tax you should be paying, and the superannuation you should be receiving. You can then compare this against your payslip.

2. **Your super fund reflects your employer's SG contributions.**
   Log in to your super fund app or website to confirm the amounts paid into your super account line up with the

amounts reflected on your payslip. As an example, if your base annual salary in the 2024–25 financial year is $60,000, your fortnightly taxable income is $2307.69 and your fortnightly SG is $265.38. So if your employer pays super monthly, you should see the amount of $530.76 paid into your super fund. If paid quarterly, the amount should be $1725.

You are also able to check super contributions that have been paid into your super fund by your employer by logging on to ATO services online via your myGov account. The following table sets out when SG payments are due with the ATO.

Due dates for super payments and ATO lodgements

Quarter	Period	Payment due date for super funds	Lodgement due date with the ATO
1	1 July–30 September	28 October	28 November
2	1 October–31 December	28 January	28 February
3	1 January–31 March	28 April	28 May
4	1 April–30 June	28 July	28 August

Payday superannuation is coming

Note that the schedule shown in the preceding table won't exist for too much longer. As of 1 July 2026, compulsory superannuation contributions will have to be paid at the same time as the related salary and wages. This change, known as *payday superannuation*, is not coming in until 2026 to allow employers, super funds and payroll providers enough time to ready their systems – quarterly payments have been the standard for literally decades.

Payday superannuation makes sense when you think about it. For your employer to pay all your package entitlements – wages and super – as you've earned them makes it so much easier to keep track. The change has an additional fiscal benefit: to be paid your super on a fortnightly basis (as opposed to quarterly), means you'll be around 1.5 per cent better off at retirement.

Taking action if your payslip and super fund don't align

After checking your payslip and your super fund, perhaps you've noticed some super amounts don't seem to have come across from your employer into your fund, or maybe the calculations don't quite make sense to you. My first recommendation is to check with your employer, if you feel comfortable speaking to them. Ask them how often they're currently paying your super, which super fund they're paying into and how much they are paying.

If you're not satisfied with your employer's responses, you can report recently unpaid super via the ATO website – just go to ato.gov.au and search 'report unpaid super' to get started. On the ATO reporting form, you'll need to enter:

- your personal details – including your tax file number (TFN)
- the period of your enquiry
- your employer's details, including their ABN.

You'll receive a receipt number regarding your inquiry once you make your submission. When your case is picked up, the ATO will ask whether you would like to keep your identity confidential.

If you need further encouragement, note that lodging an enquiry with the ATO certainly seems to be effective. Over the course of the 2022–23 tax year, the ATO raised enquiries into missing SG contributions for 175,500 employees, resulting in $379 million collectively for those people.

If these 379 million compelling reasons aren't enough to motivate you to chase up your super, remember the following:

- The missing superannuation payments are money that is owed to you.
- This money will be worth a lot more over time.

Let's look at an example to really see this in action. Let's say an employee, we'll call her Kelly, was supposed to be earning $359.10 per fortnight in SG contributions from her employer (see Kelly's payslip below).

Kelly's payslip with superannuation highlighted

Bookipi
ABN: 91617668155
George Street
Sydney NSW 2000

Name:	**Kelly Rowland**			Period starting	17 Dec 2022
Address:	5 George Street			Period ending	30 Dec 2022
	North Strathfield NSW 2137			Payment date	06 Jan 2023
				Gross earning	$3,420.00
				Net pay	$1,777.00
				Superannuation	**$359.10**

	Units	Rate	This pay	YTD
SALARY & WAGE				
Ordinary hours	76	$45.0000	$3,240.00	$33,750.00
Termination payment				
Unused long service leave				$684.00
Leave payment				
Annual leave				$450.00
			$3,240.00	$34,884.00
DEDUCTIONS				
Post-tax deductions (Workplace Giving)			$36.00	$324.00
			$36.00	$324.00
TAX				
PAYG			$1,607.00	$16,023.00
Tax on unused leave				$321.00

After two quarters – six months – have elapsed, Kelly logs in to check her super balance and realises that the SG amounts shown on her payslips for the six months have not made it in to her super fund. If Kelly doesn't pick this up, this represents $9336.60 missing from her superannuation account over a 12-month period. Added to an average super balance of $50,000, and if we assume absolutely no other contributions to her super fund from that point onwards, the total amount in her fund after 25 years, at an annual return of 6.1 per cent net of fees, will be $228,871, according to the Moneysmart calculator. Now let's add in that missing super, changing the initial deposit amount to $59,336.60. Holding all other variables the same, the new total after 25 years is $271,606. The growth of each of these balances over the 25 years is shown in the following figure.

Kelly's super balance after 25 years with missing SG contributions, versus missing SG contributions added in

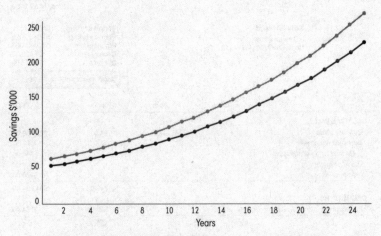

- Initial deposit of $59,336 + total interest of $212,270 = total savings of **$271,606**
- Initial deposit of $50,000 + total interest of $178,871 = total savings of **$228,871**

You may remember Linda Evangelista, supermodel of super-models from the late 1980s to early 1990s. In an interview printed in the October 1990 issue of *Vogue*, Evangelista said that she and fellow 'super' Christy Turlington had a motto: 'We don't wake up for less than $10,000 a day'.

Well, Kelly just earned herself an 'extra' $42,735 in her super fund as a result of an hour's work spent checking her super balance, talking to her employer, and lodging a missing super enquiry. Now, we could argue about whether it's 'extra' money or simply money that is rightfully hers. Either way, she earned four times that of one day's work by a great supermodel; I think Linda would be amazed! Right now, Kelly is a rich woman in every sense of the word.

Locking in salary sacrifice contributions

You and your employer can agree on a salary sacrifice arrangement – also known as salary packaging or total remuneration packaging – where you exchange part of your salary or wages for benefits of a similar value.

Put another way, instead of having your salary or wages paid to your bank account, you can have the equivalent amount paid, before tax, into your super. This lowers your taxable income, meaning you pay less tax. Not only that, but these contributions – known as concessional (pre-tax) contributions – are also taxed in your super fund at 15 per cent, which is generally less than your marginal tax rate.

For the avoidance of doubt, note the following: less salary-into-bank via salary sacrifice does not mean fewer hours worked. Salary sacrifice super contributions do not impact the ordinary time earnings (OTE) on which your employer calculates your super entitlement.

Additionally – and this is very important – salary sacrifice super contributions do not count towards the amount of SG contributions your employer is required to make. Your employer may not take advantage of your willingness to adopt salary sacrifice in a bid to lessen the amount of SG payable to you. In other words, if your employer needs to pay you $500 per month in SG, and your salary sacrifice comes to $200 per month, this does not mean your employer reduces your SG payable to $300 per month. In such an arrangement, your superannuation fund should receive the SG and your salary sacrifice: $500 + $200 = $700 per month.

A salary sacrifice arrangement also can't include:

- leave entitlements
- bonuses
- commissions.

However, other than pre-tax contributions, salary sacrifice can include:

- fringe benefits (payment of school fees, loan repayment, provision of a motor vehicle)
- exempt benefits (work-related items such as computer software, a briefcase or a laptop).

Jumping back to my exercise analogy, perhaps you can think of salary sacrifice as similar to an SAS bootcamp, where the fitness, dedication, training and skills you learn set you up for life.

Let's look at a worked example of how salary sacrifice can make you a lean, mean fighting machine.

Lynne earns $7500 per month before tax, and decides she can live on just $7000. She asks her employer to pay $500 from her salary each month – just under 7 per cent of her monthly wage – in to her super fund as salary sacrifice. Over the course of a year, this is $6000 of additional super contributions above and beyond her SG.

Quick sidebar: how did she request this salary sacrifice? Via a five-minute email, no less.

Lynne's email to her human resources manager:

Hi HR Manager

Can you please deduct $500 per month from my salary, and send it to the same super fund to which you're sending my SG contributions.

Let me know if I need to complete any other documentation for this request to take effect.

I would like this salary sacrifice arrangement to take effect from the next pay cycle, which takes place on the [day/month].

Please confirm this has no effect on the employer super guarantee amounts you currently send to the fund.

Kind regards

How does this change Lynne's taxable income and tax paid? The following table provides a quick comparison.

Total tax paid with and without salary sacrifice

	Without salary sacrifice	With salary sacrifice
Assessable income	$90,000	$84,000
Tax payable	$19,717	$17,677
Salary sacrifice	$0	$6000
Tax payable on salary sacrifice	$0	$900
Total tax payable	$19,717	$18,577

You can see the benefits straightaway:

- Lynne's tax payable has decreased by $1140 – yay!
- Lynne has increased her super contributions by an extra $6000 for that year – double yay!

Let's revert to our trusty Moneysmart calculator to see the impact that one year of salary sacrifice has had on Lynne's super balance. For the purposes of this example, let's continue to assume no further contributions to her starting balance of $50,000. Let's also retain our 25-year time horizon, and the growth rate of 6.1 per cent per annum, net of fees. The balances with and without the $6000 salary sacrifice amount are shown in the following figure.

Super balances after 25 years with and without salary sacrifice

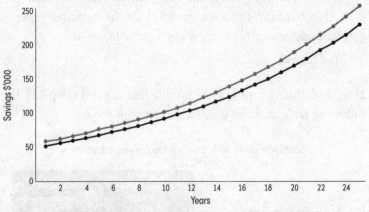

- Initial deposit of $56,000 + total interest of $200,336 = total savings of **$256,336**
- Initial deposit of $50,000 + total interest of $178,871 = total savings of **$228,871**

The difference between the two scenarios is $27,465, which is roughly equal to the cost of one year of modest living in retirement – as outlined in the ASFA Retirement Standard covered in chapter 3. Lynne's annual salary of $90,000 is pretty close to the average Australian woman's full-time salary. So, we can extrapolate from this example to create a general rule, assuming a minimum 25-year time horizon, where:

> *1 year of salary sacrifice now = 1 year of retirement living expenses*

And the best thing about salary sacrifice is the simplicity of it all. All Lynne had to do was use the email template provided on page 115, and her employer did the rest. How's that for supercharging your super?

Is salary sacrifice a 'set and forget' strategy? Absolutely. Once set up – and you have crosschecked the new additional monies are coming in to your fund each month – you can relieve yourself of the mental load from that point on.

Using matching if available

Matching was a lot more popular a decade or more ago, but it's still worth checking with your employer whether they do it.

Matching works as follows: if you add extra to your super, either pre-tax (in the form of salary sacrifice, as covered in the previous section) or post-tax (from your take-home pay), your employer will also contribute a certain percentage extra. Again, any matching contributions by your employer do not count towards the SG contributions your employer is required to make.

Matching is yet another way to supercharge your super.

As an example, the following table outlines an Australian mining company's employee matching contribution policy from 1 July 2024.

Employee Matching Contribution Policy

Employee regular contribution rate		Regular contribution rate p.a.*
After-tax p.a.	Before-tax p.a.	
0.00%	0.00%	11.5%
2.00%	2.35%	12.00%
3.00%	3.53%	14.00% (max.)

* Rate includes the superannuation guarantee for this period.

This policy means that if you contributed an extra 2 per cent post-tax, or 2.35 per cent of your pre-tax salary to your super, your company would add an extra 0.5 per cent to its SG contributions for you. Even better, if you contributed an extra 3 per cent post-tax, or 3.53 per cent pre-tax to your super, your company would add up to an extra 2.5 per cent to its SG contributions for you. To be clear, this extra super is coming from your employer's pocket. So if this option were available to you, why would you not take it?

To implement matching if available to you, use a similar email to the salary sacrifice email template provided in the previous section.

Again, matching is a 'set and forget strategy' – just don't forget to crosscheck the new additional monies coming in to your fund each month. After that, you can put your feet up and relax.

Contributing to your super if you're self-employed

If you're self-employed, the super buck stops with you. No-one else is making super contributions on your behalf, so if you don't, your super balance may end up looking pretty bleak. Of course, with all your responsibilities and other payments due, super contributions can slip further and further down the list of priorities. And, depending on the type of business you have, you may be hoping your business *is* your super – you'll sell the business for $5 million and live happily ever after! Unicorns aside, the trick is to think of the business as if it were owned by someone else. Would you work for a business where your superannuation was not being paid? No – I don't think so. In not paying yourself super, you're only robbing Peter to pay Paul.

As always, small contributions now can make a huge difference by retirement.

You have two options for making these personal contributions – either a regular transfer into your super fund, or a lump sum transfer when you have the cash. In keeping with my 'set and forget' theme, I highly recommend the first option of making small regular transfers, such as every week, fortnight or month. If cash flow can sometimes be an issue, however, transfer lump sums when you can – just make sure you do.

The great news is you can claim these payments as concessional – that is, before tax. To claim a tax deduction for these contributions, you first need to send a 'Notice of intent to claim' form to your super fund and receive an acknowledgement back from them. You also need to be aware of the current concessional contributions cap – from 1 July 2024, the cap is $30,000.

For more information in this area, go to the ATO website (ato.gov.au) and search 'personal super contributions'.

Supercharging your super outside the work environment

So in this chapter, I've covered what and how you can streamline your super contributions if you're in paid employment. But what about some set and forget strategies outside of the workplace?

Note that when I say 'outside the workplace' strategies, I certainly don't mean you have to be unemployed in order to take advantage of them. What I mean is that you can find other parties, apart from your employer, to do the hard work of making super contributions for you. This is, of course, what rich women do.

This is where Grow My Money again comes in – check out chapter 12 to find out all about it.

Who's your mate? Automate

'Set and forget' is really another way of saying 'automate'. And what is automation? Effectively, it's elimination of banal and repetitive tasks – and using 'round-ups' is a great example of this. Rounding up the total when you shop is one way to automate extra contributions to your super. In this section, I outline how this works.

First, you need to set your round-up amount – for example, you might determine that for every $9 you spend, $1 goes into your super. Setting up the round-up functionality is pretty simple – especially if your super fund offers round-ups. You connect your everyday bank account (or other account of your choosing) to your super account, set the round-up amount, and the rest happens automatically.

So, rather than you having to remember to top up your super each month with an additional $100 in the form of a non-concessional contribution, you can achieve the same outcome through simply putting round-ups into place.

While round-ups are becoming increasingly commonplace among bank providers – including ANZ, ING, and Up Bank – a handful of super funds also offer the service. Check directly with your super fund to see if they do.

If your fund doesn't offer round-ups, or if you want to mitigate against the variability that comes with round-ups – for example, one month you might have $20 worth of round-ups, another month might be $40 depending on your expenditure – then you can always set up an automatic direct debit, specifying an amount to be paid into your super and when, such as weekly, fortnightly or monthly.

Note that these contributions are non-concessional (after-tax), and you don't need to notify your fund before making them. The cap for these contributions for the 2024–25 tax year is $120,000.

Rich woman strategy

Rich women know that the best time to set up your direct debits –
as you would for any rent or mortgage payments, for example – is
on, or just after, pay day. After all, you won't miss what you never
had… and your super will be all the healthier for it.

Chapter 7

Super hacks for your 20s

The best time of your life, physically speaking, is usually during the years following high school. Whether you've gone on to university, started an apprenticeship or entered the workforce – or perhaps even started your own business – there's often no other time in your life quite like it.

You may be living at home, or flatting with friends. Perhaps you're on campus at college. Living expenses overall are usually relatively low. Certainly, these expenses end up being low compared to those that are coming your way – think childcare costs, increased grocery costs and school fees. Hopefully, during your 20s you're fairly carefree when it comes to life's responsibilities.

The best part is often the socialising. Free from the constraints of a school routine and perhaps no longer living with your parents, you're now an adult. Your social life is likely a whirlwind, filled with coffee meet-ups, brunches, lunches, dinners, parties, clubs, gigs and concerts. All that mingling probably keeps you very busy, with some late nights or early mornings. As a 20 year old (or thereabouts), it is entirely possible to only have four hours sleep and then still put in a full day's work the next day.

While you may overdo it on the eating and drinking fronts reasonably regularly, your body recovers from any excesses pretty quickly. It's great to have youth on your side. Fitness at this age and stage of your life is easier too; put in a bit of effort every once in a while, and you'll still likely see and feel the results.

As you age, though, fitness and recovery become a little harder. The head hurts more after a night out, limbs start to creak and groan, and the thought of less than six hours sleep per night for most people (except new parents) is the stuff of nightmares. Similarly, on the fitness front, you need to make fitness a regular part of your weekly routine, with increases in frequency and duration over time likely necessary to get the same results.

Now I'm going to let you in on a secret. Your 20s and 30s are the best (and easiest) time of your life to put in the hard yards with superannuation. This is again similar to exercise – if you exercise consistently in these decades, you'll be in better shape from a health perspective for when your 40s and 50s roll around. And even a small amount of effort in these years can provide big returns.

If you're doing all the right things with superannuation in your 20s and 30s, you could be a millionaire by the time you retire. No, these aren't empty promises; I'm going to show you how it can be done through this and the following chapter by presenting you with worked examples.

Before we dive in, I want you to remember that the hacks spelled out for the different decades in this chapter and the next chapter are a loose guide. For example, some women may have children in their 20s – or 40s – rather than their 30s. Perhaps you downsize in your 50s, rather than 60s. In short, I don't want you to think of these decades as a rigid construct; these hacks are suggestions based on your life stage and what's happening within it, rather than being defined by the actual number.

Super hacks as you start earning

Did I mention that your 20s are the best time in your life? Technically they're not – the best time in your life was when you were a baby, and you (hopefully) were fed regularly, slept a lot and had others coo endlessly over you! So let's rephrase that: your 20s are the best time in your life that you're able to take advantage of. You're likely earning an income, even if part-time or casual, and you may still be living with your parents, who may or may not be charging you rent. If you're not living at home, you might be living with housemates, which tends to lessen the financial load. Many 20-somethings have a digital side hustle, which generates extra income too. Generally, your disposable income is quite healthy, enabling a social life, wardrobe updates and regular holidays.

This period of your life is, without a doubt, the best time to get a head start on your superannuation.

In the previous chapter, I provided a nifty table covering the different super contribution options. Of those, the most relevant for you when you're in your 20s are shown in the following table.

Super contributions to focus on in your 20s

Type	Contribution	Summary
Employer	Superannuation guarantee (SG)	Your employer pays this to your super fund
Employer	Salary sacrifice	Extra pre-tax salary dollars you can contribute (if self-employed, you make these payments yourself)
Employer	Matching	Extra super contributions made by your employer should you contribute extra to your super, either pre- or post-tax

'Urrgh', I hear you say, 'do I really need to utilise all of these strategies? Am I really going to deprive myself of socialising or a new outfit in order to contribute to my super?' Well, the short answer is that you don't have to do anything. But if you want to become a rich woman, then yes, you will utilise as many of the superannuation strategies available to you to do so.

Let's look at the maths.

Locking in the superannuation guarantee

Vy is fresh out of her nursing degree and has started full-time work at a local hospital. Aged 23, she lives with her family, and while she doesn't pay rent, she likes to contribute to the household by buying dinner for the family once a week. Her salary is $76,000 per annum plus super. Vy is aware that the healthcare industry has one of the biggest gender pay gaps for women for average total remuneration; the Workplace Gender Equality Agency (WGEA) Data Explorer shows the gap in this sector (health care and social assistance, in hospitals) stood at 16.3 per cent for 2022–23. (The WGEA Data Explorer provides insights into individual employer's workplace gender equality performance, and allows you to compare results across different sectors and employer groups. Check it out at wgea.gov.au/data-statistics/data-explorer.)

Vy's also planning on having a family at some point in the future, and knows that a return to part-time work as a nurse is highly compatible with family and domestic responsibilities. Knowing these future possibilities, Vy wants to build as much superannuation as she can now, while she's earning a full-time wage. She already has a $10,000 starting super balance as a result of her part-time work and casual jobs during school and uni. She's also been able to pay down her student debt and outstanding

HECS-HELP loan, so doesn't have repayments being taken out of her taxable income.

Let's look at how much Vy could retire on, assuming a retirement age of 65, average net return of 6.1 per cent per annum, and no additional contributions over time – in other words, if she just relied on her superannuation guarantee. Let's also assume that, taking in her time out of the workforce for having children and the years working part-time, she has 12 years of little or no SG – making it 30 years she works full-time. For the sake of the modelling, let's hold her salary steady over the length of her career; not realistic I know, but the point of doing so will be illustrated shortly.

The online Pay Calculator tool (paycalculator.com.au) provides an easy breakdown of her fortnightly take-home pay and SG contributions. Based on her annual income of $76,000, Vy's fortnightly take-home pay is $2341.08 and her SG contribution is $336.15. The following table outlines Vy's fortnightly and annual rates.

Vy's fortnightly and annual pay, tax and superannuation figures on an annual income of $76,000

	Fortnightly	Annually
Pay	$2341.08	$60,868.08
Taxable income	$2923.08	$76,000.00
Superannuation guarantee	$336.15	$8740.00
Tax	$582.00	$15,132
Estimated tax return		–$0.01

Note: All Pay Calculator figures are estimates based on 2024–25 tax rates and government policies at the time of writing.

To calculate where Vy will end up in terms of her superannuation balance, I've again used the Moneysmart retirement planner calculator – in this case, because it offers flexibility in terms of factoring in career breaks, and making additional super contributions. For her relationship status, I selected the 'single' option – although, she may well partner. Again, we may hope for the best, but we want to plan for the worst. (Note, at the time of writing the calculator doesn't reflect the option of fortnightly, rather than monthly, SG contributions. This option is effective from 1 July 2026.)

As shown in the figure overleaf, only relying on her employer SG contributions gives Vy a respectable super balance by age 65 of $354,541. The variables entered to reach this figure are as follows:

- Age: 23
- Income: $76,000 per year + SG
- Desired retirement age: 65
- Relationship status: Single
- Starting super balance: $10,000
- Employer contributions: 12 per cent
- Additional contributions: No
- Career break for children: 01/01/2030 to 01/01/2042

According to the Moneysmart calculators, this balance of $354,541 translates to an annual retirement income of $48,456, making use of income from the super balance and the Age Pension. This amount allows for a 'modest' retirement lifestyle, as defined by ASFA (refer to chapter 3 – and remembering, of course, that ASFA's figures do not factor in rent or mortgage payments).

In fact, with ASFA's threshold at the time of writing of $32,915 being needed for a single person to fund a modest retirement, you could probably say Vy's annual retirement income is generously modest. You can refer to chapter 3 for a quick reminder of what a modest and a comfortable retirement lifestyle looks like.

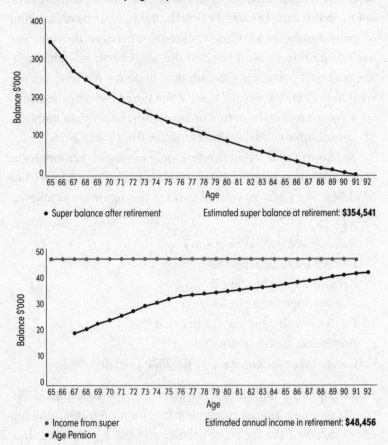

Vy's super balance at retirement and retirement income relying only on SG contributions

• Super balance after retirement   Estimated super balance at retirement: **$354,541**

• Income from super   Estimated annual income in retirement: **$48,456**
• Age Pension

Starting early with salary sacrificing

Now, Vy is clearly a smart cookie – she's thinking ahead to those career breaks already. Remember the 7 Ps from chapter 5 – proper prior planning prevents piss poor performance? Vy, at 23, is embodying this principle to her very core. She, therefore, opts to add a $200 salary sacrifice contribution per fortnight.

According to the Pay Calculator tool, her take home pay is now $2205.08 per fortnight and her combined super contributions are $536.15. And because her salary sacrifice contributions are before-tax, she's also reduced her tax paid for the fortnight – from $582 to $518. Vy's fortnight and annual figures after this change are shown in the following table.

Vy's fortnightly and annual pay, tax and superannuation figures with salary sacrificing

	Fortnightly	Annually
Pay	$2205.08	$57,356.00
Taxable income	$2723.08	$70,800.00
Superannuation guarantee	$336.15	$8740.00
Reportable contributions	$200.00	$5200.00
Tax	$518.00	$13,444.00
Estimated tax return		–$0.01

Note: All Pay Calculator figures are estimates based on 2024–25 tax rates and government policies at the time of writing.

What do her super results look like now? Again, I've assumed her income stays the same until her retirement at age 65. As shown in the figure overleaf, her super balance has been boosted to $553,183, which would provide $53,918 income per month, using a combination of the super balance and the Age pension. This is now in ASFA's 'comfortable' retirement bracket for a single person at the time of writing, for which the threshold is $51,630.

The variables entered to reach these figures are as follows:

- Age: 23
- Income: $76,000 per year + SG

- Desired retirement age: 65
- Relationship status: Single
- Starting super balance: $10,000
- Employer contributions: 12 per cent
- Before-tax additional contributions: $200 per fortnight
- Career break for children: 01/01/2030 to 01/01/2042

Vy's super balance at retirement and retirement income with additional salary sacrifice contributions

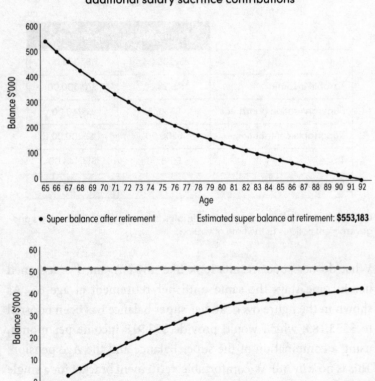

- Super balance after retirement

Estimated super balance at retirement: **$553,183**

- Income from super
- Age Pension

Estimated annual income in retirement: **$53,918**

I appreciate it's not realistic to expect Vy would limit her salary sacrifice to $200 per fortnight over 30 years; instead, she would likely increase this amount as her pay increased over time. The point I'm making, however, is this: the net total of her fortnightly salary sacrifice contributions over the 30-year period is $156,000 – yet it has yielded her $198,671. She's gained an extra $42,671 from invested the funds in her superannuation.

Adding in personal contributions

Now let's calculate what Vy's 'cherry-on-top' version looks like if she adds a little extra by way of personal super contributions. Vy's parents tell her they would rather she redirected her weekly family dinner monies in to her super. She now directs an additional $75 per week ($150 per fortnight) of her take-home pay (which is after-tax money) to her superannuation.

Rich woman strategy

Vy has followed the rich woman strategy of redirecting both sets of money into her super – her pre-tax money is being paid in directly by her employer and her post-tax money is being directed via direct debit. This means both sets of money are reaching their destination – Vy's super balance – before she has the opportunity to spend them. Because here is one thing I know to be true: *You don't miss what you never had.*

If those monies don't reach her bank account, all temptation to use them in a different way – a night out or another pair of shoes – is completely removed. With the money not available via a simple tap of a card or phone, it simply can't be spent. While salary sacrifice and personal contributions may feel like a form of forced saving, rich women get over that feeling pretty quickly once they see their super balance accelerating.

Back to Vy. I understand it's not realistic to think the $75 weekly cost of dinner wouldn't change over time – Vy likely wouldn't get much of a family meal for that amount in a decade's time (#costofliving). However, this is an illustration only, and you'll soon see why I'm holding all figures constant.

So what does Vy's pay look like now? She'll still receive $2205.08 per fortnight and pay $518.00 in tax. However, in making the voluntary contribution to her super, she can claim a tax deduction for these payments, meaning she is now on track for a $1268.00 tax return, as shown in the following table. Again, all figures are according to the Pay Calculator tool – go to the website to have a play and see the workings behind all estimates provided.

Vy's fortnightly and annual pay, tax and superannuation figures with salary sacrificing and voluntary contributions

	Fortnightly	Annually
Pay	$2205.08	$58,604.00
Taxable income	$2723.08	$66,900.00
Superannuation guarantee	$336.15	$8740.00
Reportable contributions	$200.00	$5200.00
Voluntary contributions	$150.00	$3900.00
Tax	$518.00	$12,196.00
Estimated tax return		$1268.00

Note: All Pay Calculator figures are estimates based on 2024–25 tax rates and government policies at the time of writing.

Meanwhile, back at the superannuation ranch, Vy's numbers look pretty damn good, if you ask me – as shown in the following figures. Her super balance is now $729,617, which gives her an annual retirement income of $58,541, or over $1000 per week.

The variables entered to reach these figures are as follows:

- Age: 23
- Income: $76,000 per year + SG
- Desired retirement age: 65
- Relationship status: Single
- Starting super balance: $10,000
- Employer contributions: 12 per cent
- Before-tax additional contributions: $200 per fortnight
- After-tax additional contributions: $150 per fortnight
- Career break for children: 01/01/2030 to 01/01/2042

Vy's super balance at retirement and retirement income with additional salary sacrifice contributions and personal contributions

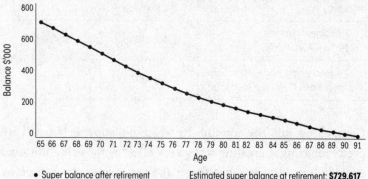

- Super balance after retirement   Estimated super balance at retirement: **$729,617**

- Income from super   Estimated annual income in retirement: **$58,541**
- Age Pension

Comparing results

You can see from the worked examples in the preceding sections that Vy's biggest advantage – other than making some smart decisions – is the time line available to her until her retirement. However, her other big advantage is consistency; she continues making salary sacrifice and personal contributions week in and week out, year in and year out.

The following table provides a summary of the three scenarios for Vy.

Comparing Vy's super outcomes

Contributions	Superannuation balance	Extra at retirement
SG only	$354,541	–
SG + salary sacrifice ($200 per fortnight)	$553,183	$198,642
SG + salary sacrifice + personal contributions ($150 per fortnight)	$729,617	$176,434

Compelling, no? The amounts by which her super is boosted are pretty amazing – creating a stacking effect with each additional contribution. *And* let's not forget the tax savings she can enjoy along the way too.

Don't forget, I included some fairly wild assumptions for the purposes of illustrating how much each of the three contribution types could stack up. These included:

· no salary increase
· no increase to salary sacrifice
· no increase to personal contributions.

All of these elements would likely increase over the course of her working life.

Micro movements equal macro changes

I also promised to illustrate how you could become a million-aire through your super contributions. So, let's make some small adjustments to each of Vy's available contributions (SG, salary sacrifice and personal). The figure below shows the results from these small tweaks.

The variables entered are as follows:

· Age: 23
· Income: $76,000 per year + SG
· Desired retirement age: 65
· Relationship status: Single
· Starting super balance: $10,000
· Employer contributions: 14 per cent
· Before-tax additional contributions: $400 per fortnight
· After-tax additional contributions: $173 per fortnight
· Career break for children: 01/01/2030 to 01/01/2042

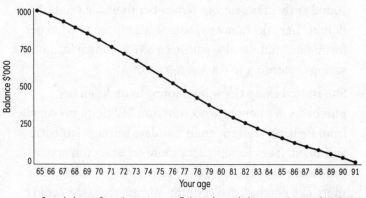

Vy's super balance after additional changes to contributions

Super balance after retirement — Estimated super balance at retirement: **$1,048,208**

Ta-dah! Vy now has a super balance at retirement of $1,048,208, *without* adjusting the figures for any salary increase over the course of her career.

What changed to supercharge Vy's super balance up from $728,824? Let's take a closer look at these very simple tweaks:

- **Vy negotiated for her SG contributions to increase from 12 per cent to 14 per cent.** How did she do this? She renegotiated her employment contract with her employer and effectively swapped out five days of annual leave – equivalent to one week of leave – for the extra 2 per cent of employer contributions. Yes, it's possible to negotiate this with your employer. Vy then planned ahead (of course!) and made use of the public holidays available to her to ensure she still had four weeks of leave. For inspiration on how you can similarly make better use of public holidays, see the seek.com.au article 'Turn your 2024 annual leave into nearly triple the days off'.

- **She increased her salary sacrifice amount from $200 per fortnight to $400 per fortnight.** An increase of $200 may sound fairly dramatic, but remember these are pre-tax dollars. Her take home pay was only reduced by $136 per fortnight – and she also enjoyed a $3120 annual income tax saving (according to Pay Calculator).

- **She started using Grow My Money to make all her purchases.** Vy bought groceries from MilkRun, pet supplies from Petbarn, booked family holidays through Expedia, and so on. (See chapter 12 for more on using this app to contribute to your super, and participating retailers.) In short, she purchased everything and anything she could through the platform, including making purchases on behalf of other family members. This ensured an extra $50 per month as an after-tax contribution to her super, taking her annual total personal contributions to $4500.

Using Pay Calculator to flow the numbers through, Vy's extra contributions to her super mean she will receive an estimated annual tax refund of $1551.50. Her fortnightly and annual figures from all changes are shown in the table below – again, go to paycalculator.com.au to have a play with your own adjustments and see the workings behind all estimates provided.

Can you believe that an entry-level graduate, in one of the lowest paid industry sectors with one of the biggest gender gaps could become a millionaire? If Vy can do it, so can you.

Vy's fortnightly and annual pay, tax and superannuation figures with salary sacrificing and voluntary contributions bumped up with Grow My Money

	Fortnightly	Annually
Pay	$2069.08	$55,346.50*
Annual income after voluntary super		$50,843.50
Taxable income	$2523.08	$61,100.00
Superannuation guarantee	$336.15	$8740.00
Reportable contributions	$473.08	$12,300.00
Voluntary contributions	$173.08	$4500.00
Tax	$454.00	$10,256.50
Estimated tax return		**$1551.50**

Note: All Pay Calculator figures are estimates based on 2024–25 tax rates and government policies at the time of writing.

* Annual pay includes all other income/loss, allowances and capital gains. It doesn't include deductions or voluntary super. This calculator is an estimate.

Chapter 8

Super hacks for your 30s to your 60s

Once you hit your 30s, it's time to consolidate some of the work you started in your 20s. Perhaps these years have an extra dimension for you, in that you've taken time away from paid employment to have children. In this chapter, I take you through some super options for this stage in your life.

If your 20s and 30s are behind you, don't worry. I also provide some hacks in this chapter to help you build your super in your 40s, 50s and even 60s.

Again, I've included the age decades in this chapter as a loose guide. Use the hacks based on your life stage and where you are with your super, rather than based on a strict age bracket.

Super hacks in your 30s

The super hacks for your 30s are really just more of the same as in your 20s, of course! However, this decade likely has one key difference, and that is the time you spend out of the workforce as a result of having children. As covered in chapter 2, time women have spent out of paid employment has historically come at a cost to their careers, savings and superannuation balances. The hacks in this section are all about filling in the gaps those career breaks have created.

I also acknowledge you may choose not to or may not be able to have children. Research from 2018 from the federal government's Australian Institute of Family Studies put the cost of raising one child for low-income families at $8840 per year – or $159,120 over 18 years. However, 2013 research from Professor Ben Phillips at the University of Canberra, published by AMP in its *Cost of Kids* report, shows a higher figure, giving the cost of raising two children ranging from $474,000 to more than $1,097,000 over their total childhood. You may choose to not have children for other reasons, including environmental and sustainability concerns, or having them might just not work out. While the actual total costs depend on many factors, there's no denying kids add another line item to your weekly budget. More and more couples are choosing not put themselves under that financial strain, and we're seeing that in the declining birth rate.

The birth rate in Australia is on a consistently downward trend – statistics from the ABS show total births in 2022 were 300,684, compared to 309,582 in 2012, a fall of almost 3 per cent. These statistics also show the 2022 fertility rate was 1.63 – below what is called the 'replacement' level; if it weren't for immigration, Australia's population levels would be declining.

Despite these overall trends, roughly 300,000 women are choosing to have children every year. What do they do about their super while they are out of the workforce?

Although it's been a couple of decades in the making, the government has finally introduced a new policy of continuing superannuation contributions while on government-funded paid parental leave, to come into effect from 1 July 2025 – hooray! But you can also take advantage of other measures to receive superannuation contributions, despite stepping out of the workforce to raise the next generation of taxpayers. The following table outlines the super tools available on this front.

Super contribution options to take advantage of when not working

Type	Contribution	Summary*
Government	Co-contribution	For every post-tax dollar up to $1000, the government may contribute $0.50
Government	Low income super tax offset	For those who earn less than $37,000 per annum, the government may contribute up to $500
Member	Tax offset	You can claim a tax offset of up to $540 per year if you make a super contribution on behalf of your spouse (married or de facto) if their income is below $40,000

*All details correct at time of writing.

The co-contribution and low income super tax offset (LISTO) are not impacted by the government payment of superannuation while you're on paid parental leave. You can utilise LISTO and the government co-contribution together in the same tax year, because they relate to before-tax and after-tax strategies. Please check the qualifying criteria for each strategy to confirm your eligibility.

Let's continue with Vy's example from the previous chapter. She starts having children at 30; due to the time spent raising the children and while her kids aren't old enough for her to return to work full-time, she is not in the paid workforce at the same level as she was before for 12 years. She does, however, work an average of 12 hours per week over a couple of shifts through those 12 years, in order to keep in touch with the nursing world, as well as give her a chance to have some adult conversation.

As I've covered, Vy is fairly on top of her superannuation. During these years of raising children, she utilises both the government co-contribution and LISTO to help plug the gap, while she is not making SG, salary sacrifice or personal contributions (to the same extent she was while in full-time paid work). Vy's partner also comes on board via *spousal contributions*.

The following sections outline how Vy leverages the strategies available to her.

Adding in LISTO

Vy's salary is now $24,000 per annum, from 12 hours paid work per week, so she now qualifies for the LISTO. (The threshold for this is $37,000.) The government automatically contributes $500 to Vy's super account once she completes her annual tax return.

Government co-contribution

Vy continues to use Grow My Money, which I explain in detail in chapter 12. The amount she is spending via the app, now that she has children, has increased substantially. She's also linked her partner's debit and credit cards to her Grow My Money account so that whenever he spends, the cashback from his purchasing comes into her Grow My Money account (this is perfectly legitimate, by the way).

As a result, Vy is now earning $80 per month in cashback from Grow My Money retailers paid directly into her superannuation, making a total of $960 of after-tax personal contributions into her super fund. The Grow My Money team pays these automatically into her fund on her behalf, so Vy doesn't have to worry about anything.

When Vy lodges her tax return, the ATO works out if she is eligible for a super co-contribution, and then pays 50 cents for each $1 she has added to her super as a result of using Grow My Money. In this example, this means an additional $480 in her super. The lower income threshold for receiving the co-contribution in the 2024–25 tax year is $45,400, while the middle income threshold is $60,400; the co-contribution remains capped at $500 regardless of whether you're at the lower or higher threshold. Vy's salary is now comfortably within the lower income threshold, and she meets all the other eligible criteria. As the government has her tax file number (TFN), they pay the $500 automatically to her super account when assessing her tax lodgement. This makes a total of $1440 per annum that Vy is contributing to her super account each year through her personal contributions, via Grow My Money, and the government co-contribution.

Spousal contributions

Vy's partner, Josh, is totally on board with supporting Vy's missed superannuation while she's raising their children. Josh contributes $2900 to Vy's super each year. Because Vy's income is below $40,000 (the threshold for the 2024–25 tax year), Josh is entitled to a $522 tax offset – in other words, a $522 deduction from his tax bill. (Josh can contribute up to $3000 to receive the maximum tax offset of $540, meaning any contributions above $3000 do not provide any more tax savings for Josh.) Note that the spouse making the contribution cannot also be that person's employer – that is, Vy cannot be employed by Josh.

Josh could also split up to 85 per cent of his concessional (before-tax) contributions with Vy under the spouse splitting option, but given her salary is less than $40,000, the spouse contribution and tax offset is the better approach for them. Make sure you check out all the other eligible criteria to understand spouse splitting. For more information on these options, go to the ATO website – ato.gov.au – and search 'spouse contributions'.

Adding it all together

Combining Vy's LISTO, government co-contribution and spousal contributions for the year gives her a total of $4840 extra going into her super. Over the 12 years she works part-time, the total additional contributions made to her super through these three strategies comes to $58,080. The following table outlines this in more detail.

Vy's combined LISTO, government co-contribution
and spousal contributions

Contribution	1 year	Total after 12 years
LISTO	$500	$6000
Personal and government co-contributions	$1440	$17,280
Spouse contributions	$2900	$34,800
Total	$4840	$58,080

The spousal contribution is the biggest contributor by far, being around twice that of the next largest (personal and government co-contributions). Had Vy remained in the workforce full-time, her SG contributions would have totalled $109,440 over the 12-year period. Her average salary of $24,000 over these years would mean she was receiving SG contributions of $2760 annually, or $33,120 over the 12 years. This brings her total contributions to $91,200 – a good result, but she is missing out on a good chunk of the super she would have earned otherwise. So when your partner grumbles about contributing to your super, just remind him or her of how much super you're forgoing by not being able to work full-time.

And the difference taking an interest in and contributing to your super while not in full-time employment makes? Let's say Vy has accrued a super balance of $150,000 by the time she goes on parental leave at the age of 30, thanks to her SG contributions, salary sacrifice and personal contributions. For the purposes of this illustration, let's also ignore the SG contributions she receives as a result of her part-time hours.

Making an annual contribution of $4840 – thanks to her co-contribution, LISTO and spousal strategies – over the 12 years results in her super balance moving from $150,000 to $387,393, compared to $305,264 had she not done anything with her super in those years, as shown in the following figure. That's $82,129 worth of uplift – over two years' worth of a modest retirement – all by utilising the 'free' money available to her, and some help from her (full-time-wage-earning) partner.

Difference to super balance with annual contribution of $4840 over 12 years, versus no contribution

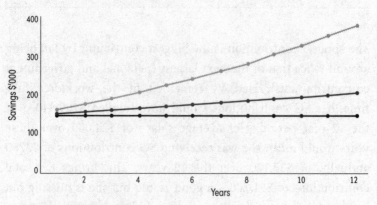

• Initial deposit: **$150,000**
• Regular deposits: **$58,080**
• Total interest at 6.10% annually: **$179,313**

Total savings: **$387,393**

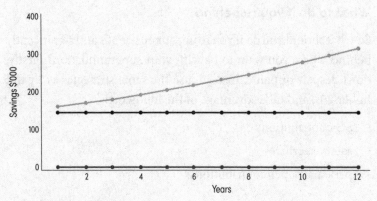

- Initial deposit: **$150,000**
- Regular deposits: **$0**
- Total interest at 6.10% annually: **$155,264**

Total savings: **$305,264**

Super hacks in your 40s

Ideally, once you enter your 40s you're using the building blocks from your 20s and 30s. If you stepped out of the workforce to raise children, now is likely the time you're stepping back in.

A funny thing happens for many women when it comes to their 40s and super. If they haven't previously taken much of an interest in their super, they typically do so around this time. The reason for this is correlated with some kind of life event, which may be any or a combination of the following:

- separation
- divorce
- death
- the last of the children commencing school.

Even the act of turning 40 can be a prompt for many; it's as though retirement is now visible on the horizon.

What to do if you're behind

So what should you do if you're in your 40s or 50s and significantly behind where you want to be with your superannuation? Firstly, don't despair or panic. Instead, use the same strategies as Vy did in her 20s, and take advantage of the following:

- SG contributions
- salary sacrifice
- personal super contributions.

In your case, however, you need to be looking at making higher levels of contributions than Vy did.

I understand only too well how hard this may be, particularly if you're juggling all the other challenges life throws at you. These may include:

- mortgage payments
- school fees
- significant health or dental bills that fall outside of insurance cover
- costs of caring for elderly parents.

People in their 40s are known as the 'sandwich' generation for a reason. At this age, they're often sandwiched between looking after the older generation in the form of ailing parents and caring for the younger generation. I know, this period in life can be the exact opposite of fun – but this too shall pass.

Back to what you need to do – focus on the following:

1. **Ask your employer if they do matching.** This wasn't the case for Vy, but it may be the case for you. Remember – if you don't ask, you don't get; the worst your employer can say is 'no'.

2. **Increase your SG contributions.** In Vy's example, she negotiated her SG contributions up from 12 per cent to 14 per cent, in exchange for reduced annual leave. You may need to increase this number further, to make up for lost time. Or, you could negotiate that instead of the variability of a bonus figure, you would be happy with a certain fixed amount into your super every month.

3. **Increase your salary sacrifice.** Vy increased her salary sacrifice to $400 per fortnight; you may need to make it even more if you're trying to play catch-up. Remember that in doing so, you're reducing your taxable income and may even generate a tax refund for yourself in the process.

4. **Continue making those personal contributions.** You can do this in a number of ways, for example, by:

    · contributing part or all of any bonuses received

    · contributing part or all of any windfall, such as an inheritance or lottery win

    · using schemes such as Grow My Money (see chapter 12)

    · using a round-up service (set up via your bank – refer to chapter 6)

    · setting up a direct debit to contribute a certain amount of your take-home pay into your super each fortnight or month.

Investing in a session with a qualified financial planner is also worthwhile. They can crosscheck your calculations, and possibly suggest other ways to boost your super balance – for example, by:

· reducing your taxable income by taking advantage of other incentives offered by the government

· increasing your contributions for your super even more.

Super hacks in your 50s

At the risk of sounding repetitive, in your 50s you need to be doing more of the same as what you were doing in your 40s:

- Ask your employer about matching.
- Contribute as much SG as you can.
- Salary sacrifice as much as you can.
- Make as much as you can in the way of personal contributions.

A lot of people I meet ask about contribution caps or thresholds. At the time of writing, the annual concessional (pre-tax) contribution threshold is $30,000. So for the 2024–25 tax year, your concessional contributions – including SG and salary sacrifice contributions – are limited to $30,000. For you to breach this threshold as a result of your SG contributions – even if, let's say, they're at 15 per cent – you would need to be on a salary of $200,000 – which is more than twice the average woman's full-time salary. In other words, this applies to a relatively small percentage of the female population. Where the contribution threshold does become more relevant is when a bonus or inheritance comes in to play.

Interestingly, I've also found that people who raise this concern (of breaching the contribution cap) with me are completely taken aback when I suggest that they still add to their super as an after-tax contribution. Sure, the contribution is taxed at a different rate – up to 48 per cent rather than 15 per cent – but it's still a contribution. And it's a contribution that reduces their taxable income and may mean they're eligible for a tax refund. Their reaction never fails to surprise me – their mentality seems to be 'concessional contribution or nothing!'

These non-concessional (after-tax) contributions still have a cap – of $120,000, from 1 July 2024. While contributions made via strategies such as Grow My Money cashback earnings and round ups won't threaten this barrier, something like a bonus or inheritance may mean you breach this cap. Again, there aren't any penalties if you do; you will just have to pay more tax.

This could also be the decade when you sell the family home and leverage the downsizer contribution, which you're eligible to take advantage of once you're 55 or older. Perhaps you had children early and they have now all flown the nest. With the kids gone, you and your partner may be rattling around in a dwelling too large for you both. You're keen to move to a smaller property, so you decide to sell your existing abode. According to the ATO, you and your partner can each make a $300,000 contribution to your super from the proceeds of the property sale. Note that this is a one-off contribution – you won't be able to contribute $300,000 over a series of years. If you can do this in your 50s rather than in your 60s, then that's a nice big lump sum that can be earning compound interest in your super for longer.

The downsizer contribution is treated as a non-concessional contribution, but it doesn't count towards your contribution cap of $120,000. However, downsizer contributions count towards your transfer balance cap, which applies when you move your super savings into retirement phase and is linked to your eligibility for the age pension. Again, I strongly recommend seeking financial advice before making this move.

Super hacks in your 60s

Can you guess what I'm going to say here? That's right – ratchet up the amounts you add to your super via:

- matching
- SG contributions
- salary sacrifice
- personal contributions.

If you haven't already leveraged the downsizer contribution (covered in the previous section), now is the time to do so. Remember that the longer your money has to earn compound interest in your super, the better.

Super hacks through the ages

To summarise the hacks covered in this chapter and the previous chapter, the following table outlines the various super contribution types. This time, I've added a column covering when those particular strategies are most relevant. While some super contribution types are relevant at all ages, others, such as government co-contribution and downsizer, are relevant at particular times of your life.

Super contributions and strategies for different ages

Type	Contribution	Summary*	Decades most relevant
Employer	Superannuation guarantee (SG)	Your employer pays this to your super fund	20s, 30s, 40s, 50s, 60s
Employer	Salary sacrifice	Extra pre-tax salary dollars you can contribute (if self-employed, you make these payments yourself)	20s, 30s, 40s, 50s, 60s
Employer	Matching	Extra super contributions made by your employer should you contribute extra to your super, either pre- or post-tax	20s, 30s, 40s, 50s, 60s
Government	Co-contribution^	For every post-tax dollar up to $1000, the government may contribute $0.50.	20s, 30s, 40s

Type	Contribution	Summary*	Decades most relevant
Government	Low income super tax offset^	For those who earn less than $37,000 per annum, the government may contribute up to $500	20s, 30s, 40s
Member	Personal	You can contribute any of your take-home pay to your super at any time (up to the non-concessional contributions cap)	20s, 30s, 40s, 50s, 60s
Member	Tax offset	You can claim a tax offset of up to $540 per year if you make a super contribution on behalf of your spouse (married or de facto) if their income is below $40,000	20s, 30s, 40s
Member	Downsizer	This is a one-off contribution you can make, when transferring the proceeds of the sale of your home into your super fund (up to a maximum of $300,000 per spouse)	50s, 60s
Member	Spouse	You can split your employer or personal contributions made in the previous income year with your spouse	20s, 30s, 40s, 50s, 60s
Member	Catch-up contributions	If your super balance is under $500,000, you can make contributions to use any missed portion of your concessional cap over the last 5 years	20s, 30s, 40s, 50s, 60s

*All details correct at time of writing.
^These initiatives are designed to support those on low incomes or no incomes; check your eligibility.

Rich woman strategy

Remember, the difference between a poor woman and rich woman is taking action – now. In particular, a rich woman takes advantage of:

- consistency
- time to retirement
- every form of 'free money' available through the strategies outlined in this chapter.

Chapter 9

Implementing your super plan

Remember the 7 Ps I mentioned in chapter 5? Proper prior planning prevents piss poor performance. I cannot stress enough how important it is to prepare now for your retirement. This is a marathon, not a sprint – and you need to pace yourself accordingly. Key factors in your marathon prep are knowing:

- the distance of the course – that is, the likely duration of your retirement
- how much training is required before – what you need to focus on to build your super balance target
- key training milestones – at which points you're able to take advantage of certain strategies, such as increasing salary sacrifice or making a downsizer contribution.

In a marathon, as in life, s*** happens. If you've trained and planned for the race, however, you'll be able to accommodate most speedbumps, dodging them neatly rather than letting them trip you up. The same is true of superannuation; if you have good super habits and a clear plan, life's curveballs should only inflict minimal damage.

Becoming a rich woman in three easy steps

In the following sections, I revisit the steps to retirement planning I outlined in chapter 4, adding in the extra details and greater insights you should now be able to bring to your plan this far into the book. All these steps are predicated around the fact that we're just considering *your* superannuation. You may be partnered as you go into retirement and therefore will enjoy some considerable cost-of-living savings. But, again, your best bet is to plan as if you will be single. You may be fortunate enough to own a property or have some other investments: perhaps you have an investment property or assets that are generating an income for you. These all form part of the wider financial picture, which interacts with superannuation.

While the topic of investments outside of super is the subject for another book, I recommend you think about what will happen to these other assets and liabilities when you're in retirement. Will you need to clear any debt on that investment property? If you sell it, sure you'll clear the debt but then you'll have less income. What happens if your partner dies just before you reach retirement? There are many difficult conversations to be had to address these scenarios. For now, let's focus on the superannuation plan.

Remember – you're going to be pulling together your three-step plan for retirement in that space of time you have carved out for yourself back in chapter 5. And, in case you missed your initial appointment with yourself, you've also blocked out two other chunks of time in which to pull this all together. Ideally, complete this planning during daytime hours, when you're feeling fresh and can make phone calls should you need, rather than after business hours when you're feeling wiped out.

Step 1, part 1

In chapter 4, I advised pulling together a draft budget of how much you think you'll need in retirement. If you haven't created that yet, or if you skipped the rest of the book to come straight to this chapter, don't worry. This section helps you really focus on this vital topic.

Remember, this retirement is unique to you and, therefore, only you can create it. Your version of retirement might look like driving around Australia without a fixed route or destinations. In contrast, I'm hoping to do a number of language immersion courses in various countries – see how different our ideas of retirement are?

While you may procrastinate about this process, I can guarantee you this:

Having your retirement budget in place provides peace of mind. You've turned an unknown into a known – and, therefore, reduced risk and uncertainty.

Don't think of this budget as a chore – think of this as an opportunity. Imagine that you're painting the vision of your retirement life. You have a blank canvas in front of you. Many artists sketch their ideas out in pencil first in an underdrawing. They rarely get it right the first time so they might go through several canvases before they're ready to then begin applying the paint. Your budget can follow a similar process of adjustment and finessing.

Consider what you want your retirement to look like. You can refer back to chapter 4 for more detail, but the following table provides a quick summary, broken down into a loose categorisation of essentials in the left column, and 'optionals' in the right column.

Budgeting considerations for retirement essentials and optionals

Retirement essentials	Retirement optionals
Accommodation · Metro, beach, rural or overseas location? · With your family, in a retirement village or independently? · House, apartment or other? **Car/s** Potential costs include: · fuel · rego · insurance **Social** · What current activities do you wish to continue? · Which activities are you planning to take up? · How often will you eat out? **Insurance and services** Potential costs include: · health insurance · life insurance · critical illness support · financial advice and/or accountancy services; e.g. retirement management and estate planning **Health** Allow for 10% of your spending to be allocated towards health costs. **Shopping** Allocate 60% of your current weekly spend towards groceries and other items.	**Work** Options include: · volunteer · mentor · working in a less structured, lower commitment manner **Travel** · Geography: domestic or international? · Frequency: quarterly, yearly or other? · Accommodation: camping or hotels? **Pets** Potential costs include: · pet food · pet insurance · boarding costs while travelling · vet bills **Big-ticket items** Potential costs include: · debt repayment · first property contribution (for children) · wedding contribution

Step 1, part 2

Now you've given all this information some thought, populate or edit the retirement template available at my website (pascalehm. com.au). This template incorporates all the detail from the Moneysmart calculators and ASFA Retirement Standard guidelines, but also allows you to include some extra considerations such as:

- mortgage/rent payments
- debt repayments
- insurances
- professional services fees.

To populate my retirement template, you can use either the ASFA numbers included in the template for reference, or use your existing monthly budget as a guide. To crosscheck your figures or finesse your budget further, you can also check out online tools such as the Rest Super retirement lifestyle budget calculator – go to rest.com.au/tools-advice/tools/calculators/ budget to check it out.

Enter the number you arrived at for your annual retirement budget here.

Retirement budget per annum – version 1:

$_____

Step 1, part 3

Again, getting a sense-check on your numbers is really worthwhile. Find someone you can trust – either someone who works in the financial planning industry or perhaps an older friend who is already in retirement. (See later in this chapter for more help finding a financial adviser.) Their feedback will help you consolidate your numbers further.

Retirement budget per annum – version 2:

$_____

Life expectancy for Australian women according to the ABS is 85. Working backwards from this age to when you plan to retire, how many years of retirement do you think you'll have?

I anticipate a retirement of _____ years

Now multiply your annual retirement budget (version 2) by your anticipated retirement duration:

MY ESTIMATION OF MY SUPER REQUIREMENTS

I will need the following amount to last me in retirement:

$_____

Step 2

From the work you did in chapter 4, what is the midpoint of your super balance estimates?

INDUSTRY ESTIMATION OF MY SUPER BALANCE

The projected annual income in my retirement is:

$_____

The projected total balance for my retirement is:

$_____

Step 3

The variation between your super balance estimates and where the industry calculators estimate you'll end up will likely be quite large, as covered in chapter 4. In order to reduce this gap, you need to either:

- decrease retirement expenses, or
- maximise your super pot.

Let's tackle the second point first, because often these items are far more in your control.

Remember, as outlined in much more detail in the earlier chapters, your levers by which to maximise your super contributions, above and beyond your employer's superannuation guarantee contributions, on a regular basis are:

- salary sacrifice
- spousal contributions or spousal splitting, if applicable
- government co-contributions or LISTO, if you're a no or low income earner
- after-tax contributions through a cashback scheme such as Grow My Money
- after-tax contributions through a round-up service
- after-tax contributions through a standing direct debit.

I've already illustrated in earlier chapters the difference to your super balance when you pull some or all of these levers. The most important point to remember is that salary sacrifice and after-tax contributions can make a huge difference to your overall balance, particularly when you have time horizon of 15 years or more on your side.

To see how much you could possibly contribute into your super, and the difference these contributions could make, keep playing with the online calculators offered by sites such as Rest Super (rest.com.au), Australian Retirement Trust (australianretirement trust.com.au) or Industry SuperFunds (industrysuper.com).

Don't forget that maximising your super pot isn't just about adding more; it's also about preserving as much as you can within it. This is why there is such a huge industry focus on both:

· fund performance, and
· fees and expenses.

To illustrate the influence of performance and fees, let's look at some more examples. Say Andrea and Zali are both 40 years old and earn the same wage as experienced teachers – $140,000 per annum, before super. Their monthly SG contributions at 11.5 per cent (for the 2024–25 tax year) work out to be $1341.67. Andrea is invested in Super Fund A, which has returned an average of 7 per cent per annum over the last 10 years with expenses of 0.6 per cent per annum, making a net return of 6.4 per cent. Zali is invested in Super Fund B, which has returned an average of 6.9 per cent per annum over the last 10 years with expenses of 1 per cent per annum, making a net return of 5.9 per cent. Andrea and Zali both want to retire at 65 years old. For the sake of this example, I've assumed no salary sacrifice or additional contributions, their salaries do not change, and their starting super balance is $50,000 each.

The only variance is the overall return on their super balance, and this doesn't sound that significant, does it? After all, what difference can 0.5 per cent make? A lot, as it turns out – $102,360 worth of difference by the time they retire, as shown in the following figure. Put another way, that's over two years of retirement that Andrea doesn't have to worry about funding.

Effect of overall returns on long-term results

	Andrea	Zali
Initial deposit	$50,000	$50,000
Regular deposit	$1341	$1341
Deposit frequency	Monthly	Monthly
Compound frequency	Monthly	Monthly
Number of years	25	25
Annual interest rate	6.4%	5.9%
Total deposits	$402,300	$402,300
Total interest earned	$782,958	$680,598

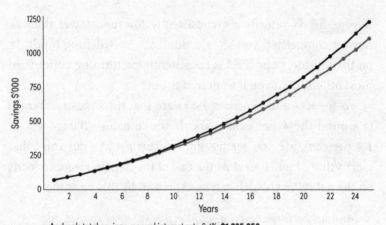

- Andrea's total savings, annual interest rate 6.4%: **$1,235,258**
- Zali's total savings, annual interest rate 5.9%: **$1,132,898**

Now, as a super fund member, you're not in a position to control the returns that the fund makes; that's up to the fund's portfolio manager. However, you are in a position to compare and contrast the performance of your fund with that of other funds. You can use online tools such as the YourSuper comparison tool (available via ATO services on your myGov account) or sites such as Canstar (canstar.com.au/superannuation), RateCity (ratecity.com.au/ superannuation) or Finder (finder.com.au/super-funds) to look at performance. See chapter 11 for more information on online tools and education options.

While you need to remember that past performance is no guarantee of future performance, your comparison exercise can highlight two things:

1. how your fund is performing compared to others in the market
2. by what margin your fund is either outperforming or underperforming others in the market.

If your fund's returns are consistently low, and lower than its nearest competitor, you should think about switching funds. If, on the flipside, your fund is consistently performing better than most others, then you'll want to stay put!

As for fees and expenses, be aware that the industry average is around the 1 per cent mark. If you're being charged 1.3 or 1.4 per cent, are you seeing outperformance by your fund that merits those higher fees? At the end of the day, you want to focus on the net return, which can be expressed by this equation:

Annual performance – annual expenses = net return

Some of the super fund comparison tools mentioned earlier – such as Canstar's – also show you what annual fees on a $50,000 balance would be, to help give you a sense of the dollar amount involved.

Again, you can't control what your fund charges – but know that the Australian Prudential Regulation Authority (APRA) is on a mission to keep the super funds honest when it comes to continually pushing them to decrease fees and expenses. What you can do as an individual is vote with your feet if you think your fund's expenses are too high – and by voting with your feet, I mean switching to another fund.

Remember to use your judgement here. What some people think of as 'high', others don't… it all comes back to the value being delivered. If you're paying 1.5 per cent in fees, but the annual return is 11.5 per cent, then your net return is 10 per cent. That is a strong net return; personally, I'd likely be happy to pay the premium fees in this instance, after I'd compared the fund to other similar funds to check their net returns.

Going back to the difference between your projection of your super balance requirements and what the industry numbers say you'll achieve, keep tweaking the numbers until you reach parity.

Also, remember to consider the other main lever you can use to influence long-term performance – the lever of reducing your expenses. As an example, run the calculations again using a tool such as the Moneysmart calculator to see the difference it would make if you switched to a cheaper fund but still received the same return. (Honestly, Moneysmart should be paying me. Sadly, they're not, but their calculators are very useful.)

If you can't reach parity, then ideally you will have reduced the gap to less than 5 per cent.

Enter those revised numbers here:

MY REVISED ESTIMATE OF MY SUPER BALANCE

The projected annual income in my retirement is:

$_____

The projected total balance for my retirement is:

$_____

And now you've done the hardest part – congratulations! You have a template for how you're going to be a rich woman in retirement.

Rich woman strategy

Rich women always acknowledge and congratulate themselves on what they have achieved. A good way to do this is to create your own 'ta-dah' list – where you keep track of everything you have achieved through your day, week or focus period. Make a note of everything you complete, and you'll soon end up with a whole list of things you've achieved – and a real sense of accomplishment as you head towards your retirement goal.

Sense-check: is your plan really... you?

You've figured out the theory and the numbers. Now it's time for a reality check – does your plan look like something that you can actually put into practice?

If you're someone who prioritises sustainability and living in an ethical way, does it make sense that your super account is with a fund that invests in mining companies? If your priorities are to live the best possible life that you can and really live for the moment, then how do you feel about significantly reducing your disposable income in order to salary sacrifice?

The point I'm making here is that, theory aside, your plan has to work for you in real life.

Back in chapter 5 I suggested you take some time to work out your core values, and then consider whether these aligned with your life and work choices. If you haven't yet completed this exercise, go back and do so now. Include your three core values here:

Core value #1: _____

Core value #2: _____

Core value #3: _____

Now reconcile these values with the retirement plan you've made. If one of your values is modesty, does your retirement lifestyle reflect that? What if joy were another one of your values; does the plan you've put together allow you joy, in the way that you derive it?

Check, check and check again

I've talked about sharing your retirement plan with someone else at various stages while being created. Now your plan is almost final, you should again ask someone to look over it – and, ideally at this stage, someone with qualifications. The more an outsider challenges your assumptions, the more refined your plan will become, and the better its chance of both it, and you, succeeding.

If you don't have a trusted financial adviser already, I strongly recommend seeking that assistance. 'I don't need advice to crosscheck my retirement plans', I hear you scoff. Are you sure? The benefits of seeking advice include the following:

- your plan for your retirement can be confirmed, or tweaked further
- any financial surprises (good or bad) are identified
- you have someone to keep you accountable and on track.

This last point in the preceding list is, I think, incredibly important during our busy lives. You need someone to help keep you accountable and on the path you've agreed to. Superannuation is highly unfamiliar to many of us; we would be hard-pressed to outline all the different steps and forms we need to complete to have everything in order. So let the expert, who no doubt has a customer relationship management (CRM) system to track these things, help keep you in line. Really, they play the personal trainer role in our exercise metaphor.

Receiving advice when it comes to your super brings with it another very tangible benefit – money, a lot more of it. In 2022, Aware Super surveyed 100,000 of its own members and found those who had received financial advice from the fund had an average of $150,000 more in super at retirement – that's four years' worth of a modest retirement they didn't need to fund. Similarly, at a conference I attended, the CEO of REST Super noted that their members aged 30 who seek financial advice will typically retire with an additional $240,000. If you think about the amount that 30 year old might have paid for that advice – let's say it was $2400 – then their return on investment is 100 times. What an incredible investment!

It cannot be said that the money required for a statement of advice – typically $2500 to $4000 – is unnecessary spending. It's the cost of peace of mind – and, really, what value can you put on that? **And as an added bonus,** if you seek general superannuation advice, you can claim the cost of that advice out of your super. While it may seem counterintuitive to pay for the advice from your super – the very thing that you're trying to build up – you're removing one of the barriers (cost) to you actually receiving that advice. You can, of course, choose to pay for this advice upfront as well.

So how do you find someone who is able to give you superannuation advice? I run through some options in the following sections.

Check what advice your super fund offers

With the wave of baby boomers now drawing down on their superannuation, the superannuation funds have had to step up their financial advice game. Many of them are adopting robo (digital) advice, in order to serve the ballooning numbers of members who require it. At the same superannuation conference just mentioned, one of the AustralianSuper execs illustrated this perfectly with the following:

- In the current year, 100,000 members will require transitioning-to-retirement (TTR) advice.
- The following year, 200,000 members will require that advice.
- In five years' time, that number will be 400,000.

The point is that the super funds are stockpiling financial advisers, either human or digital, who can provide comprehensive super-annuation advice.

A number of funds offer a first session free of charge; this is essentially a bit of a 'get to know you' session where your personal and financial circumstances, as well as your goals and what's important to you, are discussed. No personal financial advice is provided.

If you do want to move to the next stage, then a one-off fee needs to be paid for the preparation of a personalised Statement of Advice (SOA). The fee charged for this will vary, depending on the nature and complexity of the advice. Any fee should be agreed up front and in writing.

Finding a financial adviser from someone you know

If you're looking for a financial adviser from outside your super fund, select someone you know whose wealth and lifestyle you admire. At your next social gathering, ask them where they source their financial advice. Ask your contact further questions about the adviser in order to get a feel for whether you would be compatible with them. If the adviser seems right for you, ask your contact to make an introduction. If not, ask them if they know of others they could recommend.

Finding a financial adviser through a directory

Outside your own contacts, you can also research financial advisers online via a number of sites.

Start with the Financial Advice Association Australia (faaa. au/find-a-planner). This is the peak body representing financial advisers in Australia. All members are experienced financial planners who are required to uphold high professional and ethical standards. You can use the site to find advisers near you and also filter results by Certified Financial Planners. The FAAA site is effectively a directory; you'll have to do your own research and screening from there.

Another useful source is The Profession of Independent Financial Advisers (PIFA – pifa.org.au). They have created the Gold Standard of Independence for financial advisers in Australia. Represented by a logo featuring three gold stars, consumers can use this standard to identify independent financial advisers – that is, advisers who operate without incentives and conflicts. Some advisers have financial arrangements in place where they receive a commission, or are paid a fee, to promote a particular product or fund. In other words, the advice you're receiving may be influenced by their agendas. The PIFA Gold Standard logo identifies those advisers who don't accept such commissions or fees.

Alternatively, you might want to use a tool such as Adviser Ratings (adviserratings.com.au), which is a more commercial enterprise. Adviser Ratings helps match an adviser with the right qualifications to your specific financial advice requirements. The idea is that by asking consumers to select their adviser from the platform and then review the financial advice they receive, the site can help keep financial advisers accountable, accessible and affordable.

Picking the adviser who's right for you

Once you've narrowed down some possible adviser options – either through your own contacts or online directories – check out those options online. Here are some tips on doing your online research:

- Take a look at the adviser's website. Does it look contemporary, or does it look a bit dated? You don't want anything too showy but you do want to get the sense they know what they're doing.

- Have a look their customer reviews, usually available on the website, in detail. Do they talk about the qualities of the people servicing them (for example, 'they were so nice') or do they focus on the adviser's achievements ('they doubled my money in five years')?

- Check the year they were established to work out how long they've been operating.

- Crosscheck their ABN number, which should be available on their website, with the federal government's Australian Business Register ABN Lookup (abr.business.gov.au).

- Their Australian financial services (AFS) licence number should also be easily accessible on their site; crosscheck their licence number on the Moneysmart financial advisers register – go to moneysmart.gov.au and search 'financial advisers register'. This register can tell you where the adviser has worked, their qualifications, training and membership with professional bodies and the kinds of products they can advise on. This makes sure they're actually licensed to give you advice for superannuation – and not, for example, just provide advice on investments or life insurance.

· Also check any offsite reviews, such as those available via Google, Trustpilot or ProductReview. Do these reviews tell a different story to those on the adviser's website?

After you've completed your online research, you're now ready to have an initial meeting with the adviser you think might be right for you. Before the visit, make sure that you're not being charged for the session, and that no advice will be given during or following it. Similar to the first meeting with the super fund adviser (refer to the section 'Check what advice your super fund offers'), this visit is typically a 'meet and greet' session.

During your meeting, ask the adviser a few basic questions, such as:

· Who owns your business?

· What types of clients do you advise?

· How long have you been giving advice to other clients in my position?

· What is the fee structure for any advice you may gave?

· What's your investment philosophy?

· What's your attitude to risk when it comes to your clients?

· Are there any conflicts of interest I should know about?

· How and when can I expect communications from you?

· Which of your clients can I talk to as a point of reference?

Essentially you're looking for trust points; does this person or group feel reputable? Are they a good fit for you, in terms of understanding where you're at in life, as well as from a personality perspective? What's their track record? Hopefully, the answers you receive give you a feel for whether this adviser is right for you.

Rich woman strategy

Knowledge, like planning, is what separates a rich woman from a poor one. I'm sure you will come up with more questions in your meeting with your potential financial adviser. The thing I love about questions is that they are free – and the more you ask, the more you discover.

Chapter 10

Maintaining and updating your strategy

By now, you've done an incredible amount of work. You've:

- created your three-step plan to becoming a rich woman by designing a retirement that suits you
- crosschecked the plan aligns with your values
- sought validation of your plan by someone who is qualified.

You're ready to implement your plan. The next most valuable thing you can do is to schedule some regular check-ins with your plan. After all, you visit the dentist every six months – why wouldn't you do the same with your super?

The one constant in life is change

I learned this lesson in my mid-20s thanks to one of my work colleagues. He intoned those words in such a way as to make them profound… as though he was Yoda and was imparting one of the secrets of the universe. Oddly enough, my colleague was talking about the architectural plans of a new building, but I understood how his words could be applied more widely.

Change as the one constant is true – really, what else stays the same in life? Very little. People change, trends iterate, technology advances. And while the superannuation framework stays largely the same, albeit with the odd tweak as a result of policy changes here and there, life itself does not stay the same.

Here's a little list of superannuation-review-worthy life events:

- starting a job
- changing jobs
- being made redundant
- starting a business
- winding up a business
- selling a business
- getting married
- separating or getting divorced
- critical illness
- birth of a child
- death of a partner
- death of a parent.

Each of these events has the potential to impact your super-annuation, for better or worse, in some way. If you're in any doubt about how closely correlated life events are with superannuation, hopefully the following convinces you:

- Selling a business means your super could benefit from a CGT-free boost.*

---

* If you sell your business, you can contribute the proceeds into your superannuation under the 15-year exemption concession. The main criteria are that:

- a capital gain must arise on the disposal of the asset
- the asset disposed of must be an 'active asset'
- either the business turnover is less than $2 million, or the net value of your assets and assets of relevant associated entities is less than $6 million.

If your business meets all these criteria, then the sale of your business is exempt from capital gains tax if it has been owned for 15 years and if the owner is over 55 and about to retire, or is permanently incapacitated.

- Any life event involving employment, business or illness has the ability to either increase, decrease or cease your SG and salary sacrifice contributions.

- Getting married, separated or divorced all have implications for spousal contributions and spousal splitting.

- If you decide to have children, the birth of a child is going to impact your ability to contribute to your super if you step out of the workforce to care for the child.

- The death of a partner means that your superannuation may receive a boost if your partner nominated you the beneficiary of their super.

- The death of a parent means that some or all of any inheritance may be contributed to your super.

How many of the 12 life events in the earlier list have happened to you at some point in the last decade? Now, another question – prior to reading this book, when was the last time you reviewed, or thought about, your superannuation strategy? Joining those sets of dots then... are you now going to be more proactive around checking in with your superannuation strategy on a more regular basis, rather than waiting for one of life's big events to force you to take action? Good.

It's evolution, not revolution

Another key reason to check your super regularly is because *you* change. Putting aside those external factors that shape our superannuation – such as jobs, births, illness and deaths – internal factors can also influence your retirement plan. It's only natural that you evolve over time; you're shaped by your experiences throughout your life and that, of course, has a bearing on your mindset and outlook.

For example, let's say you were in your mid-20s when you created your first plan to become a rich woman using super-annuation. As part of your retirement budget creation, you deemed it vital to be able to eat out at fancy restaurants three times a week. However, in your mid-50s, you now find yourself with a number of serious dietary issues and you're happier to eat at home. Or perhaps you're becoming increasingly concerned about climate change and what kind of planet will be left for your children, so you've vowed to do without a car in retirement. Or, as many people find the older they become, you now need fewer material things – and value health and wellness over a new handbag, for example.

However your preferences may change, what's certain is that they *will* change. So why would you continue to provision for a premium retirement lifestyle when a more comfortable – and modest – lifestyle will do the trick?

Maintenance is everything

Let's think back to our exercise analogy. In preparation for your goal, you've changed your diet, started taking supplements, increased your fitness through other cardio activities and engaged a trainer. After reaching your goal – whether it was to lose weight for a wedding, or to achieve a target weight, or to run your first half marathon – you don't just let all your hard work slide away! Sure, you might have a few days off to recover but, having worked so hard, you need to maintain your new level of fitness.

Rich woman strategy

You've already come so far with your rich woman planning. The key is now to maintain your plan by checking in every six months or so. Let's do that right now, by scheduling six-monthly reminders into your calendar.

As part of your review, ask yourself the following:

- Has anything occurred recently in your life – such as a marriage or death – that will impact or change your superannuation outlook?
- Do you want to add or subtract any line items from your retirement budget? How do you feel about the amounts allocated to each of your activities – do they need to be increased or decreased?
- How are your projected annual income in retirement and your projected total super balance for retirement looking? (Remember to take the average of three online calculators.)
- How is your super fund performing compared to others?
- How are your super fund's fees tracking compared to others?
- Are there any super-boosting tasks you meant to action six months ago? This could include starting a round-up scheme or setting up a direct debit from your bank account into your super.
- If you're in a new tax year, can you now take advantage of spousal contributions, spousal splitting, government co-contribution or LISTO?
- Have you received a bonus through work, an inheritance or other windfall, or a pay increase, which will allow you to contribute more to your super as a lump sum, or allow you to contribute more via salary sacrifice?

Essentially, the questions in the preceding list bring together many of the main points raised throughout this book. The difference now is that you've already put your plan together, so the process of updating will take a fraction of the time it took to assemble it all in the first place.

You now know what to look for, how to compare and contrast, and how to use the resources provided. As a result, the updating process shouldn't take much longer than a couple of hours, perhaps three hours at the most. Easy-peasy! You can blitz it on a Sunday morning, and then skip along to your Sunday lunch, comfortable in the knowledge that your plan to becoming a rich woman is well in hand.

Just keep on keeping on

Another key benefit to checking in regularly is the ability to avert a crisis. An ocean liner cannot turn 90 degrees quickly; it changes course by making a series of small incremental changes. We can say the same of your superannuation; by checking in regularly and increasing your salary sacrifice here, or starting your direct debit there, you're able to fill in any gaps when it comes to your super balance. When you realise you've made some incorrect assumptions, and therefore will have a deficit of $75,000 in your super when you retire, which option do you choose?

- Option A – freak out.
- Option B – start looking for a second job.
- Option C – start preparing mentally for a miserable retirement.
- Option D – work out that to achieve another $75,000 by retirement, you need to increase your salary sacrifice by 5 per cent and increase your after-tax contributions by 10 per cent.

The answer is, of course, Option D. Because, even if you're in your 40s or 50s, you're still fortunate enough to have time on your side. Time is your friend and greatest ally when it comes to the superannuation race. And because you've created the habit of checking up on your super regularly, it's this habit that has saved you from having to seriously entertain Options A through C.

Perhaps you're already familiar with James Clear's *Atomic Habits*. If you haven't read this book, I strongly recommend you go and read it now. Clear shows readers how to improve motivation, attitude and goal-setting through simple everyday tasks. The book weaves together psychology, neuroscience and innate biology to discard bad habits and embrace the good ones. In many ways, *Atomic Habits* and this book overlap – particularly in terms of good habits when it comes to your superannuation.

Clear wrote two things that really stood out for me. Here's the first:

Habits are the compound interest of self-improvement.

Obviously the phrase 'compound interest' caught my attention in the context of superannuation. The key message here is that small changes add up over time – exactly like small investments into super.

The other concept that jumped out at me is as follows:

Improving by 1 per cent isn't particularly notable, sometimes it isn't even noticeable... If you can get 1 per cent better each day for one year, you'll end up 37 times better by the time you're done.

A 1 per cent change consistently means a 37-times improvement! Does that remind you of our friend Vy (from chapters 7 and 8) and how her planning meant that she became a millionaire in her retirement?

Two sets of eyes are better than one

If you've picked up this book and started reading at this chapter, I want to emphasise the importance of having your retirement plans crosschecked. (Skip back to the previous chapter for more on finding a financial adviser to provide this crosschecking role for you.)

The more an outsider – that is, anyone not in your head – challenges your thinking, the more refined your plan will become. The more refined your plan is, the less risk it carries – and the less risk, the better its chance of being successful.

Another set of eyes – hopefully those of a licensed financial adviser – will also mean that the chance of any surprises (particularly of the nasty kind) is eliminated or at least greatly reduced. They will also be able to provide other advice on how to structure your financial affairs so as to maximise other concessions and minimise tax.

And, if we think back to our exercise analogy, it's so much easier to train when you're training with someone. That other person can make sure you turn up for training and push you to improve constantly – and raise an eyebrow when you're considering a second bowl of ice cream.

According to the *Australian Financial Adviser Landscape 2022* report, released by Adviser Ratings, only 1.9 million Australians sought financial advice in 2021. This represented just 10.1 per cent of consumers, and was down from 13.9 per cent in 2018. The report also highlights the median ongoing fee has also increased over this period, going from $2520 to $3529 – an increase of 41 per cent. These increased fees in the wake of the Hayne Royal Commission are blamed for the declining rates of advice by consumers.

Vanguard's *How Australia Retires* report from June 2024 also highlighted that the cost of fees was the biggest barrier to seeking financial advice, according to 51 per cent of respondents. Other barriers included respondents not thinking they needed advice (27 per cent), lack of trust in advisers (20 per cent), and claiming they didn't know how to find a good adviser (15 per cent).

The report also described the expected most valuable aspects of financial advice, as follows:

- emotional support, including ensuring their money sustains them throughout life (44 per cent)
- feeling confident in retirement preparations (39 per cent)
- understanding spending limits (37 per cent)
- ensuring a comfortable retirement (36 per cent).

Advice is so important for all the reasons just outlined. However, the greatest reason of all, I believe, is the peace of mind that professional advice brings you – allowing you to feel confident about your strategy and have a clear plan.

While I'm not suggesting that you have a six-monthly review with a professional, having a review every other year, or as suggested by the adviser, is prudent. And remember that financial advice can be paid via a retainer, or as a one-off fee.

Fascinatingly, monetary benefits were ranked significantly lower than the intangible benefits: according to the Vanguard report, only 22 per cent of respondents mentioned seeking advice to protect investments during market declines and 29 per cent cited seeking advice to earn higher returns on investments.

What the? As a population, we know that seeking advice will make us feel better about our financial future, and we value this above fiscal benefits but… we're too tight to do anything about it. So we would rather worry and stress, and feel unconfident and ignorant, than spend, let's say, $3000. Talk about not being able to see the forest for the trees. Isn't it interesting – we'll hand over $15,000 for an international holiday to Fiji, Bali, Malaysia or Singapore in the pursuit of physical relaxation, yet we baulk at spending 20 per cent of that number on our financial and mental relaxation.

For those readers who are catching up, a number of options are available to you when it comes to seeking advice, including:

- seeking advice from your super fund
- sourcing a financial adviser through a recommendation
- finding a financial adviser online.

Jump back to chapter 9 for more information on each of these options, and questions you should ask any potential adviser.

For those of you still baulking at fees – while you can pay upfront, you can also pay for any superannuation advice out of your superannuation account. While this may seem counterintuitive, as covered in chapter 9, take a look at HESTA (click 'Get advice' at hesta.com.au) or Aware Super (click 'Super help & advice' at aware.com.au) as a starting point; the latter particularly gives a good overview of what is included with your membership, and then beyond that.

I have one final tip when it comes to using a financial adviser and continuing to review your retirement plan: also 'crosscheck' on your financial adviser's advice. In the same way you would seek two (or more) opinions for surgery or after being diagnosed with a significant illness, it makes sense to seek other opinions when it comes to your financial future. This is a big deal! It will likely be the most important investment of time and money that you make. So what if you receive two sets of advice that are identical? Great – you can be absolutely certain you're on the right path. Ideally, one of the advisers finds a loophole or recommends another strategy that can potentially make you even better off; in this case, the money you've spent on their fee has been worth every cent. Ultimately, seeking a second opinion only yields upside.

Chapter 11

Resources and tools

As you may have gleaned, I'm all about offering as many tips and tricks as possible to help you get where you want to go. Life is so busy in this digital age, and this is amplified if you're part of the sandwich generation. Looking after the generations above and below you only exacerbates further neglect of our super – at precisely the worst possible stage of our lives.

Ladies (and gents), we need to be efficient and we want top-quality information only.

Throughout this book, I've referenced various websites, calculators and tools where you can find further information or make quick calculations.

However, in the interests of making your journey super-efficient (see what I did there?), I've collated all those references here and I'm offering a few more. The goal is that, having read this book from cover to cover, when you return to it at some point in the future, you'll be able to look up this one chapter to find all your resources.

You're welcome.

Top platforms for learning

In the following sections, I've provided the website details for all platforms mentioned in this book. If an app is also available, I've highlighted that little detail.

Superannuation overview

To get your head around some super basics, check out the following:

- **Australian Taxation Office (ato.gov.au):** This website contains a wealth of information via hundreds of fact sheets, including breakdowns of key superannuation information. To get started, search the site for the fact sheet 'Your super basics'. The content is very user-focused, covering essentials such as 'What is superannuation?', 'How do I save super?' and 'How do I increase my super?' I tend to use the ATO website more as a resource for checking facts, figures and current thresholds, rather than as my first reference.

- **Moneysmart (moneysmart.gov.au):** This is the love child of the federal government and the Australian Securities and Investments Commission (ASIC), making it an 'official' platform for financial information. The site covers a range of key money topics, of which superannuation is just one component; you'll also find overviews on budgeting, debt, tax, shares and property. While I have used its calculators extensively throughout the book, other tools are available too.

- **Super Guru (superguru.com.au):** Created by the Association of Superannuation Funds of Australia (ASFA), the representative body of the super funds, this site positions itself as independent. It does not have any ties or links to any particular stakeholder such as the government or a super fund. Super Guru provides more in-depth information on various aspects of superannuation than Moneysmart does, and has some handy tools – a couple of which have already been referenced through this book.

· **SuperGuide (superguide.com.au):** This is an independent content-based website also providing in-depth information on superannuation, super funds, self-managed super funds (SMSFs), retirement planning and more. The content has an editorial angle to it – with information on how downsizing works, for example, or an analysis on recent policy changes. You need to subscribe to SuperGuide to access all the information, and they offer a tiered pricing structure (depending on your stage in life and the information you want to access). The good news is if you join SuperGuide using Grow My Money (see the next chapter), you can earn a cashback from your subscription paid direct into your superannuation.

How to choose a super fund

When you're getting into the nitty-gritty of choosing a super fund or switching to a new one, first have a look at the following websites and pages:

· **Moneysmart (moneysmart.gov.au/how-super-works/ choosing-a-super-fund):** This page provides an overview of what you should include in your decision-making criteria, such as performance, fees, investment options and a summary of how insurance in super works.

· **YourSuper (ato.gov.au/calculators-and-tools/super- yoursuper-comparison-tool):** The YourSuper comparison tool was created by the federal government to help you check how your fund stacks up against others included in the MySuper suite. This was one of the changes brought in after the Royal Commission into Misconduct in the Banking, Superannuation and Financial Services Industry, discussed in chapter 1. Only funds included in the MySuper range can accept employer contributions if you don't already have a super fund – that is, if you're starting your first job and so setting up your first super fund. YourSuper, available via myGov, helps you compare returns, fees and performance, using the simple 'performing' criteria – essentially a return benchmark the funds need to beat in order to qualify. This ATO fact sheet outlines how to access the tool, what it does, and how to use it to make the best super choices for you. You can also access myGov through the app.

· **Canstar (canstar.com.au/superannuation):** This page provides a comparison of super funds where you can choose more in-depth criteria to filter through available options. You can sort by industry super fund or retail super fund, longevity, best-performing or lowest fees. Canstar also applies its own star rating to each super fund, factoring in performance, fees and product features – and not all funds are awarded a star. *Note:* Canstar does include promoted funds at the top of its comparison table, and you may need to switch off the Online Partner filter to see all funds. Canstar also provides more general information on superannuation, including an overview of what to look for when selecting a super fund. Canstar offers an app for easy access.

· **Finder (finder.com.au/super-funds):** Similar to Canstar, this Finder page also provides guidance on how to choose a super fund and provides other factors to think about – such as aligning the fund with your values and what to consider at a certain age. Finder has detailed performance comparisons available, and you can sort by percentage return over one, three, five and ten years. Finder does not have a rating system. Also access Finder via their app.

- **Ratecity (ratecity.com.au/superannuation):** Similar to both Canstar and Finder, this site provides a solid overview of superannuation, together with a comparison tool for selecting super funds. I find the filter selection and fund features and tools more user-friendly than some of the other platforms. RateCity does not have a rating system.

- **Industry SuperFunds (industrysuper.com):** If you wish to select an industry super fund (designed to benefit members) as opposed to a retail fund (for commercial profit), this is a good platform to compare the range of funds available. All industry funds participate and contribute to this website, so you won't see any coverage on retail super funds here. The platform also has a lot of superannuation information for consumers, and dives into related topics such as shares, financial advice and estate planning.

Industry information for general interest

If you really want to do a deep dive into superannuation, here's where to head:

- **Treasury (treasury.gov.au/policy-topics/superannuation):** This is where it all starts. Treasury advises the federal government on all aspects of retirement income policy, including superannuation and age pension policies. It provides modelling of implications of demographic trends and government policy on households, as well as government revenue and expenditure. You can explore the (long) list of completed initiatives, including Superannuation Reforms (2016) and Your Future, Your Super (2020).

- **ASFA (superannuation.asn.au):** Pitching itself as 'the voice of superannuation', the Association of Superannuation Funds of Australia (ASFA) is the peak policy, research and advocacy body for the industry. ASFA regularly issues research reports and media releases on issues and challenges facing the industry; their consumer-facing brand, Super Guru, is referenced earlier in this chapter.

Top tools to help you with planning

Planning for your retirement obviously involves a number of facets but, first, I would recommend starting with – or refreshing – your understanding of the power of compound interest. Then you can move on to understanding how much you'll need to budget for in retirement, and therefore how much you should retire with. I cover these aspects in chapters 4 and 9 but have provided here some further tools to consider.

You can also compare how you're doing relative to other people your age – although I find this a bit redundant because, really, you only care about your outcome. If everyone around you is under water, does it make you feel better that you're under water too?

Understanding the power of compound interest

You cannot underestimate the power of compound interest so take the time now to make sure you're comfortable with it. Moneysmart's compound interest calculator (moneysmart.gov. au/budgeting/compound-interest-calculator) is great and user-friendly, while this page on Super Guru (superguru.com.au/ grow-your-super/pay-yourself-forward) really brings to light how every little contribution to your super helps. You can also access Super Guru's 'Small change, big savings' calculator from this page.

Provisioning for retirement

By and large, the guidance for your retirement income is that you should provision for anywhere between 67 and 80 per cent of your annual working income. That's quite a wide range, so it's worth understanding how those figures are derived. Spend a little time reading this blog from My Wealth Solutions (mywealthsolutions.com.au/blog/retirement/how-much-do-i-need-to-retire),   which acknowledges 67 per cent may be on the low side. An article from YourLifeChoices (yourlifechoices.com.au/retirement/how-much-should-you-spend-in-retirement) recommends 75 to 80 per cent. SuperGuide (superguide.com.au/retirement-planning/how-much-cost-live-in-retirement) takes a top-down approach to this issue, by reviewing some industry reports to see how much retirees are spending. The idea is that this can be used as a starting point for you to assess your own needs and preferences.

Also check out the following:

- As outlined in chapter 3, ASFA provides the industry standard around how much you should budget for in retirement – go to superannuation.asn.au/resources/retirement-standard to see the most recent. Keep in mind these calculations around a modest or comfortable income, by single or couple, do not factor in any rent or mortgage payments. A lot of the super funds cite the ASFA Retirement Standard in their own articles or guidance on how much you will need in retirement.

- Industry SuperFunds offers an easy-to-use calculator that provides a high-level overview of estimated retirement spending – go to industrysuper.com/retirement-info/retirement-calculators to get started. You'll be asked if you do or don't know how much annual income you'll need in retirement, and how much you plan to spend on larger expenses such as travel, home renovations and new cars in retirement. This is very much a 'big picture' type of calculator and it's at the other end of the spectrum compared to the granularity of the ASFA budget.

- REST Super has a user-friendly and interactive calculator – available at rest.com.au/tools-advice/tools/calculators/budget. You can select each individual element of your budget – including shopping, transport and medical expenses – and then use a sliding bar to estimate how much of your budget you will spend on each of these items. It's a good idea to have your current budget in front of you while you do this. If you haven't yet created one, head on over to moneysmart.gov.au/budgeting/budget-planner to do so.

- The Challenger Retire with Confidence tool (challenger.com.au/personal/retire-with-confidence/home/intro) helps you estimate how long your superannuation could last and calculate how much Age Pension you may be eligible for. However, it caters only for people aged between 60 and 80, who are either retired or retiring in the next two years.

How much super could you retire with

Of course, the Moneysmart retirement calculator (moneysmart.gov.au/retirement-income/retirement-planner) is very user-friendly, and I have used it extensively through this book. The calculator allows you to view your projected total super balance at retirement or predicted annual retirement income based on this balance; you can easily tweak your contributions to quickly see the difference in your projections. The most useful feature of this calculator is so discreet, you might miss it – you can schedule in a six-monthly review of your retirement projections using the little reminder at the bottom of your projections – just look for the 'Add to calendar' button.

I also like the Canstar retirement calculator (canstar.com.au/calculators/superannuation-retirement-calculator), which is very user-friendly and easy on the eye, it includes pictures, icons and offers an intuitive user experience. You're able to toggle easily between what's included (or not) in a basic, modest or comfortable retirement lifestyle.

From an industry perspective, I like the Industry SuperFund calculators (industrysuper.com/retirement-info/retirement-calculators/retirement-balance-projection). This website actually has an incredible range of helpful tools; in addition to the retirement balance projector calculator available via the link provided here, you can also access the following:

- retirement needs calculator
- transition to retirement calculator
- employer super calculator
- salary sacrifice calculator
- super contribution calculator.

These are in addition to a range of other more general finance-based calculators, such as pay calculator, tax calculator, tax refund calculator and Age Pension calculator. Just head to the main menu and click 'Calculators' to start exploring.

Mercer has a detailed retirement income simulator (supercalcs.com.au/ris9/mst) that demonstrates over how many years your super will last, and at which stage your Age Pension payments will commence. You can then easily adjust any of the main data points you've fed into the simulator. I really enjoyed playing with this tool, and found it very satisfying to see the chart changes live on screen as I made changes to my assumptions.

From a super fund perspective, I find the AustralianSuper calculator (australiansuper.com/tools-and-advice/calculators/super-projection-calculator) very technical, which (weirdly?) inspires confidence. It's easy to change the various inputs and see the follow-on effects. The Australian Retirement Trust calculator (australianretirementtrust.com.au/learn/tools/retirement-calculator#/personal-details/about-you) is more user-friendly and simple to use, while still allowing you to adjust your assumptions. Similarly, the REST Super calculator (rest.com.au/tools-advice/tools/calculators/superannuation-calculator) is easy to manage and the inputs are easily adjustable. A word to the wise, though – as I highlighted in chapter 4, every calculator uses different assumptions. So, keeping my salary, current super balance and after-tax contributions the same across each of the different calculators I used, I still arrived at four different projections of what my super balance would be!

I'll therefore reiterate my previous recommendation, which was to take an average of your super balance forecasts, as generated by calculators from each of the following:

- Moneysmart
- an industry body
- a super fund (any).

Transitioning into retirement

Again, transitioning into retirement could be the subject of a separate book in and of itself. Retirement isn't a place you just arrive at; few things in life are binary (up/down, on/off, pregnant/not), and retirement is certainly not one of them. A lot of planning and consideration is required, as well as contemplation of many factors.

Such factors include:

- your other non-super assets and how they interact with your super

- your access to the Age Pension and how much will you be eligible to receive – this depends on the value of your assets outside of super
- how you want to wind down your workforce participation.

If you're still working at what is called the preservation age – between 55 and 60, depending on when you were born – you're able to use a transition-to-retirement (TTR) strategy as you continue to work. Using this strategy, you can access some of your super as a supplement to your income if you want to decrease the number of hours you work each week. Alternatively, if you wish to keep on working full-time, you can use a TTR strategy as a mechanism to save on tax and turbocharge your super.

As always, our friends at Moneysmart have a great page that sets out the essentials, and which you can use as a departure point to learn more. Go to the Moneysmart website and search 'transition to retirement'.

Top tools to help you add more to your super

As I've stressed through this book, you can always do with more super – because 'I have too much super' said no-one ever! So, let me offer some quick tips and tools to help you add more to your super, other than through salary sacrifice contributions.

Firstly, make sure you have all your super. If you're part of the younger generation, you don't have to worry about this as much, thanks to the advent of what's known as 'stapling', which ensures when you move jobs, so does your super. But still, it's worth double-checking that your super from your casual job while you were at university (for example) has been reunited with the rest of your super. The ATO has a handy page that helps triage whether you think your super is lost, or if it's been returned to the ATO after lying dormant at a super fund – just go to the ATO website (ato.gov.au) and search 'keeping track of your super'. You'll then need to log in to your myGov account to track it down. If you think it will only amount to $500 or $1000, and are therefore questioning whether it's worth your effort in tracking it down, don't forget how much more that money can become in the long run thanks to compound interest.

I've also discussed consolidating your super. You wouldn't pay two sets of mobile phone bills, so why would you pay two sets of super charges? Again, the ATO has a wealth of information on how to transfer or consolidate your super – just search 'transferring or consolidating your super' on the ATO website.

Setting up a direct debit into your super fund each month with your take-home pay is going to boost that super balance in no time. Remember the key strategy? Ensure the direct debit is set up for the same day as your pay hits your bank account; that way, you'll never miss making a contribution *and* you're not tempted to spend it. Any windfalls – such as a bonus or inheritance – can be directed into your super fund as well.

And a reminder, if you currently have no or a low income, you can add more to your super with the low income super tax offset (LISTO) or the government co-contribution. Check your eligibility and refer back to chapter 8 to see why it's worth taking advantage of this 'free money' the government is handing out. As also covered in chapter 8, partners can help contribute to your super by either making a spouse contribution to your super account, or arranging for contribution splitting from their employer. Go to the ATO website (ato.gov.au) for more information on all these incentives.

If your super fund has a rounding-up service attached to it – where you can 'round up' purchase amounts and have the difference deposited into your super fund – then take advantage of it. Funds that offer this service include Raiz (raizinvest.com. au) and Spaceship (spaceship.com.au) whose 'starter' investment product, Voyager, designed as a feeder into their super fund, has a round-up service attached to it.

Round-ups work as a result of your spending; on this topic, take a look at how you can find extra money for your super by reducing your current spending. Making some minimal sacrifices – such as taking lunch from home to work each week, or walking to work instead of taking public transport – can really make a difference to your final super balance. The Industry SuperFunds' find extra money for super calculator (industrysuper.com/calculators-and-tools/calculators/find-extra-money-for-super) shows how all those savings add up.

Last, but certainly not least, a service such as Grow My Money – where you earn cashback into your super every time you spend – is incredibly useful for making your spending go further, and ensuring your super receives extra contributions month after month, without it coming from your own pocket. I tell you all about this tool in the next chapter.

Rich woman strategy

A rich woman knows where her money is going and just how it's working for her. I urge you to use each and every calculator, tool, budget and strategy available to you, in order to earn more super. Particularly, take advantage of any 'free' money that is on offer – such as LISTO or the government contribution, or partner contributions, or a cashback scheme such as Grow My Money.

Chapter 12

Grow your money

As well as the federal government incentives covered in chapter 9, another form of 'free money' is available for your super – via the Grow My Money app. Firstly, however, I must declare my interest.

A few years ago, I observed Australia faced what I would call a wicked problem. As highlighted in chapter 2, women over 55 are the fastest growing demographic of homeless people in Australia; quite a surprising fact for many people. Compounding this issue was the glacial pace of policy change; the government had been aware of the inequities facing women when it came to their super for over two decades and yet… nothing. And the problem appeared to be getting worse, not better, as Australia fell dramatically down the world gender equality ladder. According to the World Economic Forum's *Global Gender Gap Report 2023*, Australia was sitting in 38th place when it came to economic participation and opportunity, down from 12th place in 2006.

That a country as rich as ours would thank half of its population for their lifetime of service by letting them become homeless was outrageous to me, and a very undignified end to life for them. If we put a dollar value on all the unpaid work Australians do – predominantly undertaken by women – we would add another

$2.2 trillion each year to the economy, according to the PwC report *Understanding the unpaid economy* (released in 2017).

The wicked problem presented itself to me as this:

- Women retire into poverty because of a lack of superannuation.
- The lack of superannuation is caused by a mix of the gender pay gap, time out of the workforce and working part time or not at all.
- Government and industry tell women to just 'top up their super' – but with what?
- Government policy and social structures are proving intractable.

In short: women had no money for super, no way of earning money for super and no-one in charge was giving a s***. I thought there had to be another way. So I combined my knowledge of financial services, gender equality and ecommerce to create Grow My Money (originally titled Super-Rewards).

How Grow My Money works

Grow My Money is a platform where you turn your spending into superannuation contributions or mortgage payments – or both.

When you spend online or in-store from 1500 of Australia's leading retailers, the retailer pays cashback into your Grow My Money account. Grow My Money then transfers that money into any superannuation (including an SMSF) or mortgage account, as specified by you, on a monthly basis.

Once in your super fund or mortgage account, compound interest does its thing. In your superannuation, it will grow and become worth so much more. If tipped into your mortgage, it's saving interest, as well as shaving time off your mortgage.

The following figure provides a snapshot of how it works.

Turning your spending into saving with Grow My Money

1. User spends
$1000 at a retailer
such as Big W

2. Big W pays
a percentage of
the purchase to
Grow My Money

3. Grow My Money pays
a portion of percentage
earned into user's super
or mortgage

The list of participating retailers is huge, and includes Virgin Australia, Appliances Online, The Good Guys, Chemist Warehouse, Foot Locker, Petbarn, Expedia, HelloFresh and Australia Post.

You're spending the money anyway as you go about your daily life – buying groceries, purchasing pet food or booking holidays – now you can earn cashback into your superannuation as you do so. It really is a no-brainer.

Grow My Money was designed for women to help solve the gender super gap, but is open to any gender. When conceiving the idea, the archetype in my head was a stay-at-home mum with two children, who has stepped out of the workforce to raise her children. She's done the maths and worked out that by returning to work after baby #2 she is going to send the family unit backwards economically due to the high cost of childcare. So, together with her partner, they make the decision that she is going to remain at home until both children are of school age, and then she might return to part-time work to start with. She's not able to contribute to her super because she's stepped out of the paid workforce. Yet the time frame just described could mean up to a decade of missed super earnings.

At least with Grow My Money, she's still earning super when she's not in paid employment. While purchasing a new washing machine or sorting out Christmas – not to mention all the tasks in between – she's also contributing to her superannuation. With superannuation, every little bit really does help – as shown in the following figure, taken from this archetype's Grow My Money's user dashboard.

The impact of small contributions on your long-term super balance

The cashback balance figure on the left is the present-day value of cashback earnings; the number on the right shows how much those present day value earnings could be worth, when added to the super fund and compounding over 10, 20 and 30 years, based on a 7.4 per cent annual median net return.

The next figure shows an example of this user's dashboard, where you can see how much they spent, and how much was received in cashback.

Transaction amount versus cashback amount

Transactions

Retailer	Eligible	Cashback	Date	Status ⓘ
Bonds Instore	$88.46	$2.65	03 September 2024	Processed
Expedia	$9,467.68	$189.35	31 August 2024	Pending

The cashback earnings are treated as personal non-concessional contributions, for which the limit at the time of writing is $120,000 per tax year. This would equate to approximately $5 million of spending via the Grow My Money platform each year – be my guest if you'd like to give that amount of spending a go!

Using your shopping and Grow My Money your way

You can shop on Grow My Money via a few different methods, which I outline in the following sections.

Using the app or web platform to purchase via retailer websites

Over 500 retailers are anxiously (ha!) waiting to pay you cashback on purchases made on their website. Once you've signed up via growmymoney.com.au, accessing this cashback is very simple:

1. Log in to the Grow My Money app or website.
2. Select the retailer you would like to shop with – as an example, let's say The Iconic.

You can select retailers based on specific categories, example shown in the following figure.

Shop via online categories on Grow My Money

You can also choose retailers from the 'Popular' page (example shown in the following figure) or by using the search bar.

Shop via 'popular' retailers on Grow My Money

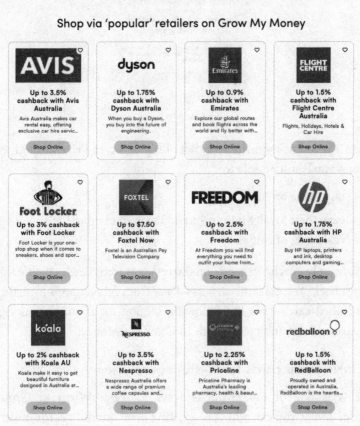

After selecting 'Shop' on the tile (shown in the following figure), you'll be redirected to the retailer's website, where you purchase your items as normal.

Shopping with your chosen retailer via Grow My Money

On The Iconic's website – or that of Big W, Myer, Priceline and so on – you'll still be able to:

· buy items on sale

· earn their loyalty points – in addition to earning the cashback, of course.

Note: only purchases made on the retailer's website are eligible for cashback. You can still earn cashback from retailer apps by using a linked card – see the following section for more on linking existing debit and credit cards to Grow My Money.

Linking your cards for in-store purchases

This is one of my favourite ways to shop. When in Grow My Money, you can add your existing debit or credit cards under

My Account – Linked Cards. You can link Visa or Mastercard cards, and personal or business accounts (#justsaying). You can add up to five linked cards.

Next, select 'In-store' in the navigation bar and browse the stores nearest you, with your location settings in your phone or laptop dictating which stores you see. Over 1000 stores nationally are ready to pay cashback when you shop with them.

As an example, let's say I go to City Extra in Circular Quay, Sydney, and spend $100 on dinner. When I pay my bill, all I do is use the card I've linked on Grow My Money and voilà! The cashback – $13 in this instance – appears in my Grow My Money account.

Linking your cards for online purchases

I think of this as the (happy) surprise aspect to Grow My Money. Because I've already linked my debit and credit cards on Grow My Money (covered in the previous section), I'm all set.

Whenever I shop at any of the participating in-store retailers listed on the Grow My Money website using my linked card, I earn cashback. I don't have to shop via Grow My Money, I can just head directly to that retailer's store, website or app. And again – like magic – the cashback appears in my Grow My Money account.

This makes Grow My Money another excellent 'set and forget' strategy for growing your super. Put very simply, here's how the 'set and forget' aspect works: when setting up your Grow My Money account, you nominate where you would like your cashback directed. To direct the money to your super fund, you'd enter the details for this fund. And then, that's it. The Grow My Money team takes care of the payments into your super account. They pay your earned cashback monthly into your superannuation, so you don't have to remember to log in and withdraw it.

All you need to think about is channelling your spending through Grow My Money's online and in-store retailers to maximise your cashback earnings.

Postscript

At the time of going to press, we are seeking investment to keep Grow My Money operational. It would be heartbreaking for me, and a loss to Australian women, if we fail to attract further investment. Should Grow My Money no longer be a going concern by the time you read this chapter, I sincerely hope that there is another similar initiative to help address the gender super gap.

Pascale Helyar-Moray
September 2024

Conclusion

Congratulations on reaching the end of this book! By now, you're rich in knowledge and know as much as I do. I've shared all my tips, knowledge and strategies with you, and hopefully you've:

- created your three-step plan to becoming a rich woman
- crosschecked the plan aligns with your values
- sought validation of your plan by someone who is qualified
- scheduled six-monthly reviews in to your diary
- scheduled reviews with your adviser every other year (or as guided otherwise by them).

To keep you motivated as you continue on your journey, I've created a summary of my main tips and tricks from this book. Remember – you have seven days of the week for exercise, so here are my seven tips to stay on top of your superannuation:

1. Substitute the word 'exercise' for 'superannuation' as much as you can to change your mindset.
2. Review your super fund performance against that of other funds (using online comparison websites).
3. Remember that your superannuation fund is just like any other provider, in that it needs to perform. If your mobile network coverage kept dropping out, you'd switch

carriers – so why not switch super funds if your fund is underperforming?

4. Check your super fund's fees and compare these to overall returns. Technology is always streamlining costs, and this should be reflected in the management cost of the fund.

5. Familiarise yourself with all the super tools at your fingertips. The resources listed in chapter 11 are a good start – but lots more are available.

6. Maximise the amount of pre-tax money you can channel to your super.

7. Stay engaged with your super – you should be comparing and reviewing at least once a year, as well as seeing if you can use any other superannuation contributions available to you.

With your superannuation retirement plan in place, you can transform your financial outlook from being overwhelmed to being in control, to reach the retirement you want, at the age you want.

You'll have also learned that I love a good story. I encourage you to send me your superannuation stories, particularly if you found that implementing any of these strategies has made a difference to your life. Of course, this is superannuation so you won't have 'quick' wins relatively speaking. However, maybe you've been inspired to change super funds and have calculated you'll be $50,000 better off simply by saving on fees. Or maybe you've already started salary sacrificing, and have just doubled your existing super balance. Whatever your story, I'd love to hear it. You can contact me at pascalehm.com.au or via LinkedIn.

I look forward to hear from you as you journey towards and reach your destination.

Glossary

ASFA Retirement Standard: an estimate from the Association of Superannuation Funds of Australia (ASFA) of how much money you'll need in retirement, depending on your lifestyle (modest or comfortable).

Age Pension: a federal government income support payment for Australian residents who have reached the required age, and meet other income and asset test requirements; at the time of writing the maximum Age Pension, including all supplements, is $1116.30 per fortnight for singles and $1682.80 for couples.

catch-up concessional contributions: larger concessional contributions you can make if you haven't used all of your concessional cap in an earlier year; unused cap amounts can be carried forward for up to five years before they expire.

compound interest: interest calculated on both the initial principal and all of the previously accumulated interest.

concessional contributions: money that goes into your super fund before it's taxed, including payments made by your employer; at the time of writing, these contributions are taxed at 15 per cent once they're in your fund.

contribution caps or *thresholds:* the maximum amount of concessional (before-tax) and non-concessional (after-tax) contributions you can contribute to your super; for the 2024–25 tax year, the concessional contributions cap is $30,000 and the non-concessional contributions cap is $120,000.

defined benefits scheme: a fund in which your retirement benefit is determined by a formula instead of being based on investment return; the benefit paid is determined not only by the money invested into the fund by you and your employer but also by factors such as your average salary before you retire and the number of years worked for the employer.

defined contributions system: a fund where contributions are paid into an individual account by you and your employer; contributions are then invested, and returns on the investments credited to the fund.

downsizer contribution: a contribution of up to $300,000 from the proceeds of the sale (or part sale) of your home into your superannuation fund; you must be 55 or older to be eligible.

endowment effect: placing more value on something you already own than you would place on that same item if you didn't own it.

environmental, social and governance (ESG) analysis: a way to assess companies and investment options on non-financial topics, such as safeguarding the environment, treatment of staff and leadership and internal controls.

equity: investment in a company via purchasing shares of that company in the stock market.

financial literacy: being able to understand and effectively use various financial skills, including personal financial management, budgeting and investing

fixed interest: an investment that offers a set rate of interest for a specified amount of time, with the principal repaid at maturity; includes term deposits, and government and corporate bonds.

gender pay gap: the difference between the average earnings of women and men, expressed as a percentage or dollar figure.

industry fund: superannuation funds run only to profit members; they don't pay profits or dividends to shareholders.

knowledge gap: an area where the necessary skills, expertise or knowledge needed to be successful are lacking.

loss aversion effect: the tendency to prefer avoiding losses over receiving an equivalent gain.

low income super tax offset (LISTO): a payment made to your super fund if you earn under a certain amount; in the 2024–25 tax year, if you earn up to $37,000, you may be eligible for a payment of up to $500.

matching contribution: an employer policy whereby employee contributions to a super fund are matched by the employer.

non-concessional contributions: payments you make into your super from your savings or from income you have already paid tax on.

payday superannuation: a requirement that employers pay employees super at the same time as their salary and wages; comes into effect from 1 July 2026.

preservation age: age you must reach before you can access your super; if born after 1 July 1964, preservation age is 60.

retail fund: superannuation funds run by banks or investment companies; they are open to anyone and often have a wide range of investment options.

risk profile: an evaluation of your willingness and ability to take investment risks; it is influenced by many factors including age, time to retirement and overall retirement goals.

salary sacrifice: where you choose to give up or 'sacrifice' part of your before-tax salary and add it directly into your super account.

self-managed super fund (SMSF): a private super fund that you manage yourself, allowing you to choose the investments and insurance; funds are subject to specific rules and responsibilities.

spousal contributions: paying money into your spouse's super from your after-tax income; if your spouse is a low-income earner, you may be able to claim a tax offset.

super co-contribution: made by the government into your super fund if you're a low- or middle-income earner and make non-concessional contributions to your fund.

superannuation guarantee (SG): the minimum amount of super employers must pay into their employees' super funds; from 1 July 2025, the SG will be 12 per cent.

transfer balance cap: the lifetime limit on the amount you can transfer into one or more retirement phase accounts.

References

Introduction

Kiyosaki, R, *Rich Dad Poor Dad*, 1997

Chapter 1

Australian Institute of Health and Welfare, 'Deaths in Australia', June 2024

Chapter 2

Australian Conciliation and Arbitration Commission, 1973

World Economic Forum, *Global Gender Gap Index*, 1996

Sweeney Research, *Westpac Kids and Money Report*

Association of Superannuation Funds of Australia, 'ASFA urges action to close the retirement savings gender gap', July 2023

Workplace Gender Equality Agency, *Gender Equality Scorecard*, 2022-2023

The Household, Income and Labour Dynamics in Australia (HILDA) Survey: Selected Findings from Waves 1 to 20, *The 17th Annual Statistical Report of the HILDA Survey*, 2022

Australian Institute of Health and Welfare, *Informal carers*, September 2023

Workplace Gender Equality Agency, *Unpaid care work and the labour market*, 2016

Australian Bureau of Statistics, *Population: Census*, 2021

Australian Consumer and Competition Commission, *Childcare inquiry 2023*, October 2023

Australian Bureau of Statistics, 'Labour Force Participation Rate', June 2024

Workplace Gender Equality Agency, *Making It A Priority*, Gender Equity Insights 2021

Parliament of Australia, '*A husband is not a retirement plan*': *achieving economic security for women in retirement*, 2016

The Mercy Foundation Australia, '*Older women and homelessness*' mercyfoundation.com.au/our-focus/ending-homelessness/older-women-and-homelessness

Australian Institute of Health and Welfare, *Specialist homelessness services annual report*, 2022-2023

Habitat for Humanity, *Hidden in plain sight: how women are experiencing homelessness*, November 2023

Faulkner, D & Lester, L, '400,000 women over 45 are at risk of homelessness in Australia', *The Conversation*, 2024, theconversation.com/400-000-women-over-45-are-at-risk-of-homelessness-in-australia-142906

The Household, Income and Labour Dynamics in Australia (HILDA) Survey: Selected Findings from Waves 1 to 21, *The 18th Annual Statistical Report of the HILDA Survey*, December 2022

Dean, L, 'Most Australians can't answer all of these five basic money questions', *Australian Financial Review*, December 2022, afr.com/wealth/personal-finance/most-australians-can-t-answer-all-of-these-five-basic-money-questions-20221130-p5c2kv

Chapter 3

Association of Superannuation Funds of Australia, 'The ASFA Retirement Standard', superannuation.asn.au/resources/retirement-standard/

Australian Bureau of Statistics, 'Main source of income at retirement', 2022-2023

Australian Institute of Health and Welfare, 'Housing Affordability', March 2023

Chapter 4

Parliament of Australia, *Retirement Income Review Final Report*, July 2020

Chapter 5

Australian Securities and Investment Commission and Beyond Blue, *Money and Mental Health Social Research Report*, August 2022

Australian Securities and Investment Commission, 'New Moneysmart data reveals young women more stressed than young men about finances, cost of living', February 2024, asic.gov.au/about-asic/news-centre/find-a-media-release/2024-releases/24-023mr-new-moneysmart-data-reveals-young-women-more-stressed-than-young-men-about-finances-cost-of-living/

OECD, *OECD/INFE 2020 International Survey of Adult Financial Literacy*

L&A Social & Pureprofile, *Social Media Census 2020: Australian Social Media Usage in 2020 and the Change in Behaviour Post COVID-19*

Australian Bureau of Statistics, 'How Australians Use Their Time', October 2022

YouGov AU, 'Half of Gen Z and Millennials in Australia have taken a social media break for their mental health', October 2023, au.yougov.com/health/articles/47536-half-of-genz-and-millennials-in-australia-have-taken-a-social-media-break-for-their-mental-health

headspace, *Young people cite social media as main reason for worsening mental health*, May 2022

Chapter 7

Workplace Gender Equality Agency, Data Explorer, wgea.gov.au/data-statistics/data-explorer

Chapter 8

Australian Institute of Family Studies, *New estimates of the costs of raising children in Australia*, April 2018

AMP.NATSEM Income and Wealth Report, *Cost of kids: the cost of raising children in Australia*, May 2013

Chapter 10

Clear, J, *Atomic Habits*, 2018

Adviser Ratings, *Australian Financial Advice Landscape*, 2022

Vanguard, *How Australia Retires*, June 2024

Chapter 12

The World Economic Forum, *Global Gender Gap Report*, June 2023

PwC Australia, *Understanding the unpaid economy*, March 2017

Acknowledgements

This book is dedicated to all the women who prioritised everyone's needs above their own when it comes to their family. Whether this was a conscious or unconscious choice, you probably would have tweaked some of your discussions and decisions, had you been aware of the financial implications of putting yourself last. To those who can change their journey's course as a result of reading this book, I ask you to share your newfound knowledge with others.

In turn, I would like to thank those who have shared their financial or business knowledge with me, either through mentoring or instruction. Whether you were an employer, a work colleague, a friend from the industry or other, please know you left an imprint: Nicolette, Kelly, Camila, Sue, Andrea, Lucinda, Nicole, DL, Yolande, Barnaby, Rob, Peter, Lisa P, Lisa G, JJ, Paul, Chris, Sandy, Fay, Elaine, Phil, JG, David, Thryth, Ness, Jasper, Campbell.

To those who share the passion for financial literacy for women and the pursuit of gender equality – particularly Marion, Alex T, Victoria, Coral, Terry, Vy, Marie, Yvonne, Tash, Canna, Nicole, Lynda, Jade, Trenna, Jenny, Sarah, Jennifer, Jacqui and Glen, not to mention Moana, Effie, Gemma and Kathryn C.

To my colleagues at Grow My Money who show up every day to fight the good fight. Ally, you turbocharge my efforts generally and for this particular project specifically. Kylie, thank you for your steadfastness and support over the years; it's fair to say I wouldn't have made it to this point without you. Randolf, Brett, Jordan, Dan, Alan, Trena, Martin, MAL – thank you. Kelly, Dale and Randall – the support you've shown has gone far above and beyond what a founder could ever expect, let alone hope for.

Alanna, your awards submission culminated in recognition which was game-changing in my internal landscape.

To my cheer squad: Lucy, Alex, Anna E, Kathryn M, Lisa D, Christina, Monica, Lex, Geri, Karen, Wendy, Jen, Alexx, Katie, Kate G, Krista, Michelle, Anna D, Marnie, Kellie, Kerrie, Penny, Anne-Marie, Tanya, AJ and Lynne. GvE, your willingness to read drafts was encouraging. Brooke, Deanne, George and Suze-the-lioness – thank you for your mental rebalancing.

To Lisa C for her accounting wisdom as well as insistence on making me pay myself superannuation (a long time ago) when I was a novice business owner. More recently, your ongoing advice and support has meant so much – thank you.

Lesley, thank you for the initial approach; 'Have you thought about writing a book?' you asked. My answer? 'Yes, because I have so many super stories to tell!'. Charlotte, thank you for bringing all those stories together. To the team at Hachette for getting onboard with the 'superannuation = broccoli' analogy.

Finally, to my family; Hugo, Charlotte and Missy who inspire me every day. To Dusty, the fur baby who faithfully kept me company during late-night writing and editing sessions. And to my husband Tim, who has supported me constantly and endlessly throughout the writing process, as well as our decades of adventures together.